see charitable Lead Trust - 8283

Rich Dad's ADVISORS™

P9-DDY-070

Real Estate Loop-Holes

Secrets of Successful Real Estate Investing

DIANE KENNEDY, C.P.A. - Tax Strategist
and GARRETT SUTTON, ESQ. - Attorney at Law

WARNER BUSINESS BOOKS™

Published by Warner Books

An AOL Time Warner Company

Mary
Thurs.
4-1-04
3:00

Copyright © 2003 by Diane Kennedy, C.P.A. and Garrett Sutton, Esq.
All rights reserved.

Published by Warner Books in association with CASHFLOW Technologies, Inc. and BI Captial, Inc.

CASHFLOW and Rich Dad are registered trademarks and Rich Dad's Advisors is a trademark of CASHFLOW Technologies, Inc. Success DNA is a registered trademark of Success DNA, Inc.

   are trademarks of CASHFLOW Technologies, Inc.

 Warner Business Books are published by Warner Books, Inc., 1271 Avenue of the Americas, New York, NY 10020

Visit our Web site at www.twbookmark.com

An AOL Time Warner Company

The Warner Business Book logo is a trademark of Warner Books, Inc.

Printed in the United States of America

First Printing: January 2003
10 9 8 7 6 5 4 3 2 1

ISBN: 0-446-69135-6
LCCN: 2002117139

Cover by Kevin Stock, ImageSupport.com, llc

My Poor Dad often said, "What you know is important." My Rich Dad said, "If you want to be rich, who you know is more important than what you know."

Rich Dad explained further saying, "Business and investing are team sports." The average investor or small-business person loses financially because they do not have a team. Instead of a team, they act as individuals who are trampled by very smart teams.

That is why the Rich Dad's Advisors book series was created. Rich Dad's Advisors will offer guidance to help you know who to look for and what kind of questions to ask so you can gather your own great team of advisors.

Other Bestselling Books by
Robert T. Kiyosaki & Sharon L. Lechter

Rich Dad Poor Dad
What The Rich Teach Their Kids About Money That The Poor And Middle Class Do Not

Rich Dad's CASHFLOW Quadrant
Rich Dad's Guide To Financial Freedom

Rich Dad's Guide to Investing
What The Rich Invest In That The Poor And Middle Class Do Not

Rich Dad's Rich Kid Smart Kid
Give Your Child A Financial Head Start

Rich Dad's Retire Young Retire Rich
How To Get Rich Quickly And Stay Rich Forever

Rich Dad's Prophecy
Why The Biggest Stock Market Crash In History Is Still Coming...
And How You Can Prepare Yourself And Profit From It!

Other Bestselling Books by Rich Dad's Advisors

Contents

Foreword   ix

Part One   **Being Smart**   1

Chapter 1   Why Invest in Real Estate? 3

Chapter 2   Being Smart with Your Real Estate

              Investment Plan 9

Chapter 3   Your Real Estate Plan 25

Part Two   **Tax Secrets**   31

Chapter 4   Introduction to Tax Secrets 33

Chapter 5   Three Types of Income 37

Chapter 6   Legal Deductions 43

Chapter 7   Tax Rate Magic 53

Chapter 8   Loophole #1: Principal Residence 57

Chapter 9   Loophole #2: Accelerating Depreciation 65

Chapter 10   Loophole #3: Real Estate Professional 69

Chapter 11   Loophole #4: Sell Now, Tax Later 75

Chapter 12   Loophole #5: Getting Money Out of

              Your Property 87

Chapter 13   Loophole #6: Real Estate Investing with

              Your Pension Plan 89

Chapter 14   Loophole #7: Tips for Qualifying for a Loan . . . 93

Part Three   **Legal Secrets**   97

Chapter 15   Homestead Exemptions 101

Chapter 16   Land Ownership and Notice Requirements . . . 105

Chapter 17   Landlord Liability 113

Chapter 18   Insurance 121

Chapter 19   Joint Tenancies/Tenancies in Common/

              Land Trusts 127

Chapter 20   How to Hold Real Estate 137

Chapter 21   Structures for Your Real Estate/Tax

                 Considerations 153

Part Four   Selection Secrets

                 Introduction to Selection Secrets 159

Chapter 22   Property Analysis 161

Chapter 23   Legal Due Diligence 169

Chapter 24   Real-Life Selection Stories 183

                 Conclusion 195

Appendix A   Frequently Asked Questions 197

Appendix B   Useful Real Estate Checklists 207

                 Buyer Disclosure Checklist 207

                 Seller Disclosure Checklist 209

                 Commercial Property Due Diligence

                    Checklist 210

                 Environmental Due Diligence

                    Checklist 212

Foreword by Robert T. Kiyosaki

Before beginning my business career, my rich dad insisted that I learn to be a real estate investor. At first, I thought he wanted me to invest in real estate simply for real estate itself. As the years went on and my base of education grew, I came to better understand the bigger picture of the world of investing. Rich dad said, "If you want to be a sophisticated investor, you must see what your eyes cannot see." What my eyes could not see were the loop holes, the legal tax advantages that real estate investing offer the more informed investor. In other words, there is far more to real estate than dirt, sticks, and bricks. This book, written by Diane Kennedy and Garrett Sutton, two of my trusted advisors, goes into the real reasons why the rich invest in real estate. *Real Estate Loopholes* will take you into the world of real estate investing the average investor rarely sees.

Today, I make my money in several different businesses. I also play the stock market and make some of my money in that market. But the bulk of my wealth is held in real estate. Yet more than store my wealth in real estate, I am able to magnify my wealth using the loopholes real estate offers the sophisticated investor. If you are ready to find out how to use legal and little known loop holes that investing in real estate offers, this book is for you.

REAL ESTATE LOOPHOLES

Part One

Being Smart

Do you want to know a secret?

Do you want to know a secret about loopholes that allows successful real estate investors to do so well?

You don't have to be a genius to understand and apply these loopholes. You just have to be willing to follow a proven path toward success. Basically, you need to be smart about following what others have used to their advantage before you.

The truth about real estate loopholes is that there are two types of them.

From a tax standpoint there are real estate loopholes to be opened. The Tax Code, as put forth by Congress and the IRS, encourages certain real estate activities. Smart investors know how to open these loopholes to their maximum advantage.

From the legal side there are real estate loopholes to be closed. There is liability and risk associated with owning real estate, leading to loopholes of increased personal liability and responsibility for the claims of others. These legal loopholes must be closed in order to gain asset protection and to best protect yourself and your family.

How can I learn these secrets, you ask? And how can I apply them?

The secrets of real estate loopholes are not handwritten on aged parchment, locked in a dark and inaccessible vault and guarded by huge rabid dogs, fed by the rich and powerful as a way to exclude all newcomers. To the contrary, although not set out everywhere, the important loophole strategies—the ones you must know—are found in the pages of this book.

In using these loopholes you have to be willing to combine the experience of others with the specifics of your own situation. This is not hard to do. In all aspects of our lives we synthesize and apply information. But unlike most other activities, by learning when to open loopholes and when to close them, you are going to significantly improve your results as a real estate investor.

And in applying these loopholes you will become smart about selecting real estate, as we will review in the final section of this book.

Let's begin by answering an interesting question . . .

Chapter 1

Why Invest in Real Estate?

We've all seen the get-rich-quick real estate ads. There is something compelling about the idea of starting with nothing (No money down!), investing just a little time (Work in your spare time!), and getting wealthy (Get rich overnight!). The systems, books, seminars, and infomercials make it seem that all you have to do is buy the right product (the one being sold!) and real estate riches will immediately and effortlessly be yours.

Real Estate Loopholes is not for someone who is looking for a get-rich-quick scheme. It is a book that provides legal and tax knowledge so you pay less tax legally and protect your real estate assets. It is for serious real estate investors who want to understand and apply the loopholes in order to increase their yields with more security. It is written by two Rich Dad's Advisors™ who, although working in their professions as an attorney and a CPA, are building their personal wealth through real estate. These techniques are practiced in their own personal lives as they continue to invest in commercial and residential real estate. Just as with any business venture, the key to finding wealth with real estate investing is through gaining knowledge, developing and following a good plan, and by building a team of advisors and mentors to provide expert guidance.

Why Real Estate Works

Investing in real estate has many lifestyle advantages over other investment strategies. You have more control over the value of your real estate holdings than you do with your shares of stock. You can update your rental property to bring in higher rents, but there's not much you can do with your stock certificates. There is also clearly more freedom involved with just letting your real estate portfolio build than there is with a regular day job or an investment strategy that keeps you glued to your computer monitor.

The benefits that are discussed in this book are primarily the tax and legal loopholes available only for real estate investing. These are the secrets that experienced investors know.

Benefit of Real Estate #1: The Leverage of Good Debt

Picture yourself walking into your local bank, Bank of Your Town, and asking for a loan of $1 million in order to buy an apartment building. You come to the meeting armed with financial projections and pro formas that show income from the apartment building can pay for the debt. With the right financial records as backup, you'll likely get the loan.

Now picture yourself walking into your local bank, Bank of Your Town, and asking for a loan of $1 million to buy stock in their bank. You come to the meeting armed with the financial projections that the bank itself has put out in its prospectus for investors. Not only would you *not* get a loan, they would likely laugh you out of the bank.

There is an ease with which you can get in the game. In other words, real estate allows you to use good debt (debt that buys assets which in turn bring you cash flow) to build a business and provide passive income. Banks, mortgage companies, insurance companies, and private parties, among others, will finance sound real estate investments run by owners with a track record of sound financial decisions.

What if your past history of financial decisions has been less than stellar? That is another one of the benefits of real estate; there are lots of ways to accomplish the purchase. There are many fine programs available that advise you on how to find seller financing. There are also programs available to help you clean up past credit problems. And, finally, there are always investors available that are interested in the high returns possible in real estate, if they can have a partner they trust who will find the deals and set up the program.

Rich Dad Tip

Good debt is debt that is used to purchase an asset that puts money in your pocket. Bad debt is debt that is used to purchase a toy or doo-dad. A real estate investment makes use of good debt.

Benefit of Real Estate #2: Secret for the Advanced Investor—Using Leverage with Appreciation

One of the biggest advantages of leverage, or good debt, is a trick of leverage that works in your favor. You might have heard the statistics about apprecia-tion in real estate. Consistently, throughout the world, we have seen growth in the value of property. Obviously there are peaks and valleys in the value of real estate, when viewed within the short term and within specific areas. For example, there is a roughly seven-year cycle in the value of real estate in some areas of California. You can see values rise and fall within that cycle. But each cycle raises the value—the highs are higher but the lows are higher as well. In the United States, the overall appreciation for the past thirty-five years has been over 6 percent.

Now here is the real magic. The entire property value rises in value. It's not just the money that you have invested that goes up—it's the bank's portion too.

Rich Dad Tip

Turn $20,000 into Millions with Real Estate!

One of the many benefits of real estate is the ability to leverage—using other people's money. Following is an astounding demonstration of how $20,000 can be turned into over $6 million in twenty years by using this abil-ity to leverage.

Here's one example that demonstrates why real estate is such a good in-vestment.

To keep it simple, some basic assumptions have been made. Overall, the assumptions are very conservative based on the real-life experiences of DKA (D. Kennedy & Associates, Certified Public Accountants) clients.

ASSUMPTIONS:

(1) Loan at 90 percent of value of property. NOTE: If you can't find a 90 percent loan (called 90 percent LTV, loan to value), keep looking. A good mortgage broker can find this loan.

(2) Zero effect cash flow with no closing costs. NOTE: Obviously, you will have closing costs. Also, if you've made a good real estate investment, you will also have the positive cash flow return. In order to keep this model simple, we have assumed that the cash flow can cover the cost of the payment, insurance, vacancy, and repairs as well as cover the closing costs.

(3) No negative tax effect. NOTE: There would be a phantom passive loss due to depreciation. This passive loss could reduce your taxes. The benefit from this passive loss has not been included in this example.

(4) The appreciation rate is assumed to be 5 percent per year.

PLAN ONE:

Buy a property for $200,000, with 10 percent down. Assume a loan of 7 percent per annum, fully amortized over thirty years.

At the end of twenty years, the property will have appreciated to $530,660. At the end of twenty years, the loan balance will have decreased to $103,142.

Your initial $20,000 investment has become $427,518 (the equity in the property). Not bad! In fact, that's a rate of return of 16.5 percent over twenty years. But you can make much, much more by using the magic of good debt.

PLAN TWO:

Step One

Buy a property for $200,000, with 10 percent down. Assume a loan of 7 percent per annum, fully amortized over thirty years.

Step Two, Five Years Later:

	Property #1
Property appreciated value:	$255,256
90 percent (available for loan):	$229,730
Note balance:	$169,437
Cash-out refinance amount:	$60,293

Buy a second property for $600,000, with $60,000 down (10 percent down using the $60,000 from your cash-out refinance).

Step Three, Five Years After Step Two:

	Property #1	Property #2
Property appreciated value:	$325,779	$765,769
90 percent (available for loan):	$293,201	$689,192
Note balance:	$216,248	$508,310
Cash-out refinance amount:	$76,953	$180,882

Buy a third property for $2,570,000 with $257,000 down (total cash-out refinance is $257,835).

Step Four, Five Years After Step Three:

	Property #1	Property #2	Property #3
Property appreciated value:	$415,786	$977,337	$3,280,044
90 percent (available for loan):	$374,207	$879,603	$2,952,039
Note balance:	$275,995	$648,748	$2,177,263
Cash-out refinance amount:	$98,212	$230,855	$774,776

Buy a fourth property for $11,030,000 with $1,103,000 down (total cash-out refinance is $1,103,843).

Step Five, Five Years After Step Four (Twenty Years After Step One):

	Property #1	Property #2	Property #3	Property #4
Property appreciated value:	$530,660	$1,247,357	$4,186,259	$14,077,386
Note balance:	$352,247	$827,984	$2,778,801	$9,344,443
Equity:	$178,413	$419,373	$1,407,458	$4,732,943

The total *equity* is now an amazing $6,738,187!

Advanced real estate investors use other people's money to grow their wealth. What if you don't have twenty years to wait for your wealth to increase? Or what if you want to start off with more, or less, than $20,000? You can develop your own personal investment plan with the Real Estate Wealth Builder calculator, for free, at www.taxloopholes.com. Please note that the above example used some rounding which will give you a slightly different answer than you would get by running the "Real Estate Wealth Builder" calculator.

Benefit of Real Estate #3: Tax Advantages of Real Estate

Another exciting advantage of real estate is the tremendous tax benefits available for the real estate investor. One of the fundamental principles in the United States has always been the advantage of the property owner. When the Constitution was first written, property ownership was the measure of voter eligibility. In other words, only property owners could vote and determine the direction of the country. Half of the measurable wealth of our country was held in property. We were set up over 200 years ago to be a country shaped by real estate owners. That's why there are so many tax loopholes written in tax law. They support the real estate investor. Congress continues to pay attention to the voting public. The many tax advantages of real estate ownership are more secure than other current tax provisions because *Congress* recognizes who votes!

Part Two, "Tax Secrets," will explain seven of the top loopholes available only for real estate investors.

How to Have a SUCCESSFUL Real Estate Investment

Of course, you want to take advantage of all the tax benefits for your real estate investments. As the value increases for your real estate investment, you will also want to protect that investment. One drawback with real estate is that it is a highly visible asset. There are unscrupulous people who might want to take that valuable property away from you. The ownership of the property also has some risks. We call them tenants. You can protect yourself against these risks. Part Three, "Legal Secrets," discusses how you can legally protect your property.

Chapter 2

Being Smart with Your Real Estate Investment Plan

Public interest in real estate investing, just like stock investing, follows trends. Right now real estate investing is popular and the how-to books abound. But the fundamentals remain constant as do, over time, the returns. There are many different ways to make money in real estate, including:

- Buying foreclosures (where to find the property)
- Buying "no money down" (a technique to buy)
- Apartment houses (type of real estate)
- Commercial (type of real estate)
- Flips (technique for making money—not cash flow)
- Lease options (technique for creating cash flow)
- Fix-up (way to create a job)
- Trailer parks (type of real estate)

Most books show ways to find property or techniques for buying, becoming self-employed, or creating cash flow. These are all examples of plans that use real estate to achieve personal goals.

What Do You Want from Real Estate?

Determine what you want from real estate. Do you want to work for your-self, instead of for others (such as with a "fix up and sell")? Do you want tax-advantaged appreciation for the future? Or do you want cash flow that just shows up each month? Real estate investing can offer you all of these things. One word of warning: Don't try to create a plan initially that does all of these things. Find what you want to concentrate on and then just do that.

It is important to first understand what you want to accomplish with your real estate investment. The plan you develop and follow should address those needs. Remember that, just like any aspect of financial planning, one size does not fit all. We all have unique circumstances, gifts, desires, and goals. Plans should be unique and customized so that you are set up to achieve the goals you want.

Product Versus Plan

One of the key distinctions that successful investors know is the difference between a product and a plan. It might seem simple, but we are inundated in today's media with the illusion that products can substitute for plans. For example, you might see various types of exercise equipment advertised on television. Those are products. They may be highly valuable and effective products, but they are useless without a plan.

The same is true for real estate products. Real estate itself is a product. It can be a good product or a bad product; it completely depends on what you do with it. There are many fine programs that advertise amazing re-sults to increase your cash flow and net worth through the use of real es-tate. In this case, they are selling a plan as a product. It may or may not work. It doesn't have anything to do with the quality of the product or its validity; whether it works depends on *you* and your personal plan for im-plementation. A startling statistic is that over two thirds of the self-help tape sets ever bought are never even opened. These are potentially life-changing tools, but the buyer never implements them, and they sit gather-ing dust on the shelf.

Make it your goal to create and follow your own plan. Take the first step, and the next, and the next. The biggest risk of all to you is your own inaction!

Real Estate Investing Versus Stock Investing

Investing in real estate and investing in stock require different skills.

You can invest in stocks by yourself. You can sit in front of a computer monitor each and every day and never have to talk to another human being. And, in fact, if you understand how to make money in markets that go up, in markets that go down, and in markets that go sideways and you know how to tell the difference, you can make a very fine living.

Real estate investing, on the other hand, requires people skills. You will need to negotiate with sellers, contractors, leasing agents, and tenants. You will have to manage a team of experts and you will need to be able to select and trust your team. Most first-time real estate investors fail because of problems relating to their relationships with other people. Listen to the typical reasons given for their investment failure: bad tenants, unscrupulous contractors, lying sellers. In all cases, the problem had to do with their relationship with people—their team. Of all skills, people skills will be the most important for the real estate investor. Building a good team is how advanced investors make smart investments.

Your Real Estate Investing Team

The fastest and most powerful results from investing in real estate come when you get help from your team along the way. There are three major steps to building an effective team:

IDENTIFYING YOUR TEAM

First, you need to identify those people who are currently acting as team members. Who currently gives you (or tries to give you) advice? Who influences the decisions you make? This question might not be as easy to answer as you first think. There are many unseen influences on our lives. In fact, there may be people who influence our life today who are long since gone. But their effect on us, sometimes traumatic, continues unseen. Start to identify all the people who influence you now and who have influenced you. Start by listing everyone you can think of who has had an influence on how you view money and your investments. Try to list at least twenty people. Tomorrow look at the list and add ten more. Continue each day until you can't think of any more people. Then the next day, add ten more names to the list. Keep that list for the next step, evaluating your team.

Now you need to identify the team members you want to have. Write down all of the specialties you will need access to for your business venture. The next several pages will discuss some of the types of team members you might need for your real estate business. Next to the type of team members you will need, list the qualities that you want them to possess. For example, if you list a real estate agent as one of the team members you want, what are the qualities that you will want in that person? As professionals, the authors appreciate when a prospective new client can tell us clearly and succinctly what they want. In some cases, our firms do not have the necessary specialties that the new client is looking for. It is helpful to know that right away and avoid wasted time and frustration.

Diane's Team

Following is the list of advisors that Richard, my husband, and I have on our team for our personal real estate investing:

- Real estate agent
- Real estate attorney
- Mortgage broker (not a loan officer)
- Insurance agent
- Real estate appraiser
- Home inspector
- Handyman
- Classified ad agent
- Escrow officer
- Cleaning person
- Bookkeeper

Your own list of advisors will likely be different, depending on your own circumstances and plan. Our team is further discussed in the next few pages.

Real Estate Agent

Richard is a licensed agent, and so we have easy access to information on good deals. Over the course of years, we have had a range of real estate investing plans, most centering around residential real estate.

When we have extra money, Richard starts looking for our next property. But more than that, Richard is always on the lookout for a great deal. A great deal for us is defined as a property that has an easily fixable problem that is deflating its current value. For example, we recently bought a condominium that was a foreclosure by Fannie Mae (a government lending program). This was at a time when the Phoenix, Arizona, market was at an all-time high. I was being told almost weekly by the nay-sayers that it was impossible to cash-flow a property in the Phoenix market. To be honest, I was fed up with hearing that excuse, because I knew it wasn't true. I went home after speaking at a seminar of real estate brokers in Phoenix who had told me the entire time that you can't find a cash flow property in Phoenix anymore. Richard and I took that as a personal challenge and at ten P.M. that night started searching the MLS (Multiple Listing Service). That's how we found this condo.

Richard looked through the MLS for properties that had been on the market for over ninety days. In the hot Phoenix market, it was highly unusual for a property to remain unsold for over a month, so ninety days was an anomaly. We had discussed this strategy before and had thought we might be able to identify the properties that had a problem that might be able to be fixed easily. An easy fix meant little time and money and the upside had to be rewarding to pass our test.

Using that criterion, he had found a Fannie Mae repossession. It was a condominium in an area that was turning into primarily rental. The problem with the property was that the government owner had no idea how to market it. In fact, they had turned off all the utilities to the property in an effort to contain costs. That meant that you had to view the property during daylight hours (not when most people look at homes) and then only see it dimly at best.

The house also had the smell of disuse. It wasn't completely unpleasant, but it wasn't a good feeling going into it. Fannie Mae did, however, offer a very attractive loan package to purchasers. We were able to buy the property with only 15 percent down and with no PMI (private mortgage insurance). Typically, PMI is required on any property that you buy with less than 20 percent down. It will add approximately 1 percent per year to the payment on the property. The property cost $31,500 and with cleaning and new paint—which we hired others to do—we were then able to rent it on the Rent to Buy™ program for $650. This gave us a cash-on-cash return of 51 percent per year. If we had done the cleaning and painting ourselves, the return would have climbed to 68 percent.

This condo project was a great example of what you can accomplish when you direct the efforts of your real estate agent. In this case, Richard, as a licensed agent, was able to search the thousands of listings with very specific criteria. It is rare to find an agent who really understands investment property. So give your real estate agent clear instructions about what you want. If she can work within those guidelines, great—you have a team member!

Real Estate Attorney

You will want to have an attorney on your team who knows the state and local rules of the real estate market in which you invest. Each state and, in many cases, city has different rules. So if, for example, you own property in Detroit and Miami, you are most likely going to want a real estate attorney in each locality.

Your attorney should be familiar with the concepts raised in Part Three of the book, "Legal Secrets," and be able to competently advise you on the state and local rules regarding such issues.

Mortgage Broker

We choose to work with a mortgage broker, as opposed to a loan officer. A mortgage broker can pick a loan program that best suits your needs. On the other hand, a loan officer is limited to the products of the company for which he works. A good mortgage broker should be able to read financial statements and tax returns. My mortgage broker is especially good at understanding the different types of business structures in which I am involved and how those affect my own borrowing capabilities.

Don't take "no" for an answer when you are applying for a loan. There are many different types of programs available today. If you are turned down for a loan, find out why and see if there is something you can do to correct the problem. Sometimes it is a problem with the mortgage broker and sometimes it is a problem with the product. Try to determine where the problem lies.

Your mortgage company rarely loans you the money directly. Usually, they sell the loan to another party. That second party is the underwriter of the loan. If you have ever experienced a loan process going great and then, at the last minute, receiving urgent requests for more information, it is likely that the underwriter has just gotten involved. The best mortgage broker will have a close relationship with their underwriters and be able to predict many of the requests for information.

Our mortgage broker, Alec, is very much in demand because, quite simply, he is that good. Alec doesn't hesitate for an instant to fire a difficult client. He reasons that his day is stressful enough without unreasonable, uncooperative, and just plain rude people. And for every request for a loan from him, there are a dozen more behind them. We make sure that he knows how much we appreciate him and promptly reply with information whenever he asks a question. In the case when he might make duplicate requests for information, like any good team member, we immediately send it over. Anything we can do to make his job easier benefits us.

Mortgage Banker—Garrett's Comments

I prefer working with a mortgage banker. The difference between a mortgage banker and a mortgage broker is the difference between dealing direct and dealing through an intermediary. A mortgage banker has their own source of funds. They are lending their money. A mortgage broker doesn't fund the deal but rather finds third-party lenders for funding.

While a mortgage broker may have many lending sources to consider, unlike a mortgage banker, they are not in charge of the decision to lend. You may find yourself in a situation where certainty is scarce at a time when financing contingencies in your offer call for decisions to be made.

Another concern when dealing with mortgage brokers has to do with fees. Because mortgage brokers are independent, they charge a finder's fee or a processing fee to obtain the loan for you. Which is fine, they are in business to make money. However, when you are dealing direct with a mortgage banker you will generally not have to pay those fees. So, using a mortgage banker may save you money in terms of fees for funding.

An example of a professional mortgage banker is Todd, who is with a large financial institution. Todd is based in Reno, Nevada, but can lend on properties throughout the United States. For Todd, the most important elements in selecting a mortgage banker have to do with confidence and empathy. A client should have confidence in the mortgage banker's level of experience and commitment to their needs. As well, a client should have a very strong sense that the mortgage banker has their best interests at heart. The mortgage banker should know their short-term and long-term goals and fully educate the client on their current and future funding options. For Todd, his clients become clients for life.

An area to watch out for, according to Todd, is whether the mortgage broker or banker uses a contract underwriter or a staff underwriter to assemble and submit the loan package. A contract underwriter is like an independent contractor. They are not day-to-day employees and, as such, may not know the parameters needed to close a deal. Their unfamiliarity can cost a potential borrower time, money, or even the deal. On the other hand, a staff underwriter is an employee of the mortgage banker and is aware of what is needed to successfully fund. They are more prone to look for reasons to close a deal.

Todd also points out that his industry is always changing. For example, Todd's company offers over 1,700 financial products and programs. Even the most professional mortgage executive cannot keep up with every single one.

So, in your search for the right mortgage banker, you need to find someone with enough experience to both know that there are hundreds of ever-changing funding options out there and to know how to access the right one for your particular situation.

Insurance Agent

We have a number of properties that include two personal residences and numerous rental properties. We work with one insurance agent who knows about all of the properties. The total insurance bill is smaller because the agent has consolidated our policies. I'm certain we get better service because we are one of his larger clients. If there is ever a question, our bookkeeper just needs to make one phone call.

Real Estate Appraiser

Our real estate appraiser is an important member of our team. She not only provides the appraisals we need for new financing and refinancing, she also has been a great source of information regarding undervalued property. For example, during a conversation a few months ago, we learned that a particular area of Phoenix was valued largely based on the square footage of the home. The appraiser told me that she could not count a downstairs basement as square footage in the living area of a certain home unless there was a bathroom. The couple living there had completely redone this historic home but found that the 1,000 square footage in the basement did not count in the total square footage. In this area, square footage went for roughly $150. In other words, this basement square footage could add a value of $150,000 to this home. The appraiser cautioned me that basement square footage was devalued somewhat by buyers. But even at a 50 percent discount of the added value, we calculated that for the cost of a $5,000 bathroom, we could add $75,000 in value to a home.

But, along with learning about this valuation deal, I also learned another lesson. You see, I talked about the great deal with many friends. Richard and I kept going back and forth, trying to decide whether to tackle another property. We took too long—someone else bought it! Sure enough, the new owners put the bathroom in downstairs and added to the value. They currently live in the house, but I know if they choose to sell it, they have picked up a lot of value. And, that gain could be tax-free if they follow the advice of Chapter 8, "Loophole #1: Principal Residence."

My appraiser has been a great source of tidbits like this one. She also has a good feel for what is happening in the real estate market and in particular areas within Phoenix. We value her comments and opinions.

Home Inspector

We include a "subject to inspection" clause in all of our property offers. We first met our home inspector when he represented the buyers for a home we were selling. He handed us five pages of necessary repairs for the almost new home we were selling. At that moment, we decided we had to hire this guy.

We now use him for all properties that we buy. He does the same thorough job, listing every defect (minor and major) in explicit detail. This is now a bargaining point for the offer that has already been accepted. We typically give the list to the seller and ask them to fix all the items. At this point, they're ready for the sale to happen and so generally offer us a lower purchase price to close the deal fast. Since we have a team in place to fix the necessary items, we always make money on the deal, knowing that we can do the work for less than they have just paid us.

Classified Ad Agent

Through trial and error, we have identified the best newspapers to advertise our properties are the smaller free weeklies. Probably because they are much smaller, their advertising agents know us, and know our properties. They call when there is a special on advertising rates, just to see if we have anything that is ready to go. They also help with the copy on the ads. They know what gets the best results from their history of working with other ads.

It is actually pretty unusual to have classified ad agents as your team members, but we were fortunate to form a couple of great relationships.

Escrow Officer

I cannot say enough good things about my escrow officer. Sherri is bright and experienced with a tough job. Most loans close within a very short window each month. The stress is incredible. Again, anything we can do to make her job easier, we do willingly.

We bought the downtown building that my CPA practice is in about three years ago. It is located within a historic district in Phoenix, Arizona. Phoenix has an attractive incentive program to encourage redevelopment in this area. There is also a 20 percent federal tax credit available for historic buildings meeting certain specifications and a 50 percent federal tax credit available for ADA (Americans with Disabilities Act) alterations. This building was going to need a lot of work, but the tax credits and city incentives made it worthwhile.

In the days just before the loan closed, I got a strange call from Sherri. She had been looking at the documents and just had a feeling that something wasn't right. She asked if we could hold up escrow for a day while she investigated a hunch. We trusted her and immediately gave our permission. The seller was anxious to unload a property that needed work and so also gave their permission to hold off one day in order to save a sale.

During that day, she discovered that the house had originally been constructed on one whole lot and one half of another lot. The title had actually conveyed that way. Sometime in the rush, and crash, of the 1980s, the property was foreclosed upon by a bank. The bank, however, had foreclosed only on the whole lot. The title to the half lot was not conveyed. The bank then collapsed and the federal government picked up the property through the Resolution Trust Corporation. The property was sold for pennies on the dollar to another party. Of course, only the whole lot conveyed. The new buyer began an aggressive fix-up project and was 90 percent done when he ran out of money. The new bank foreclosed on the property. This property was then sold to the next owner, who completed the addition and then sold it as is.

That's when Richard and I showed up. Although we thought we were buying the house and lot, we actually were only buying one lot, not the half lot that the corner of the house rested upon. Meanwhile, the half lot had been sold at a tax lien sale and someone had bought the lien. There was less than one year on the lien left to run. Once the time was up, someone else would then have legal right to the half lot.

Thanks to Sherri, this potential mess was discovered before more damage could be done. We told the seller of the problem. It was his responsibility to clean up the title and include the half lot with the property. It delayed the transaction about a month, but the knowledge that our title would be good was well worth the wait. I don't know how much the seller had to pay in legal fees and to the lien holder for the half lot, but I am glad it wasn't me!

That's just one reason why we are so loyal to our escrow officer. We insist on using her title company for all our transactions. She also understands the real estate game that we play, and why we do it. Every time we do a property transaction, she sends over the paperwork with a candy bar . . . a PayDay.

Cleaning Person

One of our rules for personal investing is that the real estate cannot take much of our personal time. It is indeed possible to buy, sell, and manage real estate without the services of a cleaning person, but we do not choose to do so. In fact, our cleaning person also serves another helpful function.

As described, we buy properties to sell under the Rent to Buy program. It is generally necessary to show the properties multiple times until we can find the right buyer-tenant. An effective way to show the property is to purposely reduce the amount of time that it is available to be seen. That means that more than one person shows up at once and it helps buyers to move more quickly. It also makes more efficient use of my team's time.

We run an ad in various weekly papers describing the program and the property. For more information, the reader is instructed to call a toll-free number. There are recorded announcements on this number. When they listen to the message, they are told of the next open house for the property. Typically, we do these open houses on Saturday or Sunday afternoon.

But remember, one of our goals is not to take a lot of our time. So we hire our cleaning person to sit the open houses. During that time, she cleans the house and directs interested people to pick up a flyer and put their name and number on a log. She calls Richard at the end of the open house to report on the names and numbers recorded. We pay her a bonus for each name on the list. From this list, we can usually find an interested party after just two or three such open houses. Meanwhile, the house is kept in great shape as our cleaning person cleans it each week.

Bookkeeper

The bookkeeper for my CPA practice also keeps the books and records for our properties. I know that this is a luxury many cannot initially afford. However, the bookkeeping requirements for real estate are some of the most difficult. And, unfortunately, many people neglect this important aspect until the rude awakening that occurs at tax time. Professional services exist to handle such needs.

If you do not have a bookkeeper on your team, you will need to learn some fundamentals of real estate bookkeeping. Don't wait until the last minute. The "Business Structure and Tax Loophole" box, available at www.realestateloopholes.com, is an excellent way to set up the accounting and legal strategies to protect your real estate investment. Above all, do not ignore this necessary part of owning real estate.

Your Individualized Team

Your team may include some of the same types of people that ours has. But everyone has unique characteristics and their team will reflect their needs and goals, so include the people *you* need to help *you* succeed in real estate investing.

EVALUATING YOUR TEAM

As with identifying your team, there are two stages to evaluating your team. First, you will want to evaluate the current team members you have listed. This is a list that is likely to be quite long. You might find that some of your advisors have many issues related to money. For example, many of us have learned our spending habits (good or bad) from our parents. They might have lived a frugal life, denying themselves pleasure, and so you respond by living life to the fullest. That involves a lot of other issues. But for now, you can identify that your parents lived a frugal life. Their belief about money was that it was scarce. So, next to each person, list the dominant qualities about money and finances that they have.

Some Common Beliefs

Some common beliefs about money: "Money is scarce." "You need to work hard to succeed." "It takes money to make money." "You have to be lucky to succeed at business." "Money is the root of all evil." "You have to make a choice between family (health, spiritual life, etc.) and business (money, success, etc.)." "You need to be debt-free to be truly rich." "Money is easy to make." "All you need is a good idea to succeed." "Build assets to build wealth."

Some common beliefs about real estate: "If you own a rental, you'll be fixing toilets at three A.M." "Renters will trash your property." "You can't find a good renter." "Property always goes up in value." "You shouldn't fall in love with an investment property. Look at the numbers first." "You need to have a lot of money to buy a property." "Owning properties takes a lot of your time."

What beliefs do you want your team members to hold?

Interview

The second stage of evaluation comes as you start to interview your prospective team members. Remember that the interview process will actually be a dual evaluation. They are looking you over, just as you are looking them over. In order for the process to work there must be a fair exchange between participants. To provide the best true exchange, ask yourself what you can do to add value to them. In some cases, with advisors, that means paying your bills timely and without complaint. With other team members, it may be a cooperative exchange of your working with them on their projects and their helping you with your projects.

You can use the DKA "Advisor Checklist" to evaluate your own advisors. This checklist is available is free at www.dkacpa.com.

BUILDING YOUR TEAM

After you have identified your prospective team members, now is the time to start building the relationship with them that will support you. One of the best ways to do that is with clear communication. Discuss what you want from the relationship and then listen to what they want. Don't do all the talking! In fact, many of these team members have been selected because they have information and experience you need. So listen to them. Remember that their way of doing business may be different from what you are used to. That is exactly why you have chosen them!

Another key fact is that as people become more successful, they have less time for the things that don't work. They divide everything into "things that work" and "things that don't work." A highly successful person simply does more of things that work and less of things that don't work than the less successful person does. Frequently, a successful mentor or advisor will have little patience for justifying or explaining why something doesn't work. Once they know it doesn't work, they move on and do something different. So be prepared for a different way of working with your new advisors; be patient, as you might not fully understand everything at first; and listen more than you talk.

Build Loyalty in Your Team

To build a loyal team, everyone needs a sense of exchange. In other words, your team members need to feel that they are receiving as much as they are giving. This doesn't necessarily mean money—it could be the free exchange of worthwhile ideas, legitimate opportunities, or simply hard work.

If you are looking for a mentor, remember that there are a lot of demands on successful people's time. They receive many offers of "let's go into partnership and I'll contribute sweat equity." The "free exchange" of work for a partnership share inevitably turns out to be the successful investor putting in just as much time as the novice, plus all the money, credit, and expertise. These are not fair exchanges and they don't work!

On the other hand, there is a great story about a cleaning lady who worked for a client. She listened and learned from this successful investor about their real estate investments. She followed their advice on a small scale with her own money. In fact, her employers didn't even know the cleaning lady was investing. It was only years later that they learned how much she had amassed. They were happy to share the knowledge and even happier to learn how she had taken advantage of the opportunity. They did not feel used, because all those years she had performed a valuable service for them. They were in exchange.

How Do I Find a Mentor?—Diane's Comments

Those were the first words out of Cassie's mouth as she met with me to discuss her plan to begin her brand-new real estate venture. "I went on a few online discussion boards and announced that I wanted a mentor and no one responded," she continued complaining. "People just don't want to help anyone anymore."

I stopped and considered her complaint. I had been asked a number of times to mentor someone. In fact, one person had even produced her whole plan to work for me in my tax strategy firm, learn from me while being paid so that she could then go out and do it herself. She had come from a nonaccounting background and had nothing to offer, plus wanted to get paid. Needless to say, I didn't take her up on her offer.

"Cassie, what do you have to offer someone else?" I asked.

"What? Nothing! I don't know anything about real estate!" she exclaimed.

"I disagree. I know your plan is to use your talent for seeing renovation possibilities, as well as your strength and determination, to rehab homes. How about volunteering to help someone who is currently doing that?" Warming to the idea, I continued with new vigor. "In fact, Cassie, you could start off right at the top and tell them that you will work a specified number of hours per week *first*. Then, tell them what you want to get from them. I suppose you could run into someone who would take your volunteer work for free and never give what was promised, but at least you'd have a shot at learning."

I stopped to see how she reacted. I knew that I was a little more emotional on this subject than normal because I'd seen so many people complain that they couldn't get mentors. They were very clear on what they expected from the experts (usually a paycheck *plus* free information). But they weren't clear at all about what they expected to give. I thought I'd let Cassie come up with her own plan, and we moved on to the estimated tax projections for her investment fund.

Why Is Advice Sometimes So Expensive?— *Garrett's Comments*

I am asked this question frequently. And having been on both sides of it—giving advice as well as paying for it—I can provide two answers:

Both have to do with the marketplace. First of all, while the market for expert services is dynamic and competitive, it is not perfect. The fact that an advisor in San Francisco, Chicago, or Philadelphia charges twice as much as that of an equally competent advisor in Reno, Springfield, or Harrisburg has less to do with what the market will bear than it does the availability of information on less expensive alternatives.

But you can overcome that information gap by using the Internet and other resources to search out the right advisor for you. Consider using the free professional directory at www.successdna.com. Remember, an advisor's price per hour is not as much a reflection of competence but rather work flow. There is a difference. If a price quote seems too high, continue your search. Know that alternatives exist.

Second, when you sense an advisor is playing games to increase their fee do not hesitate to look elsewhere. Again, the market is not perfect. Not everyone realizes that many advisor services are fairly straightforward and should not be overly expensive. This is not to deter you from assembling a team of advisors but rather to encourage you to trust your own intuition in such decision making. If you feel an advisor is manipulating your situation to generate fees, seek out a new advisor.

How Do I Know if I've Selected the Right Advisor?—Garrett's Comments

Because you have relied upon your intuition, which is probably the best people indicator you'll ever get. Yes, you have probably interviewed several people and taken measure of their experience and pricing. But above all, you've likely formed some sort of connection or sense about them that is shaping your decision.

Do you like to do business with egotistical, overbearing, and discourteous people? I don't. And I won't have them on my team. So I weed them out in favor of the keepers—the ones my intuition says to go with.

And once they're on the team, I rely on them.

Chapter 3

Your Real Estate Plan

Your Real Estate Plan

The first step to building your real estate plan is to determine what your goals are. Don't confuse the idea of having a product (owning real estate) with the idea of having a plan (creating passive income). It's easy to get lost in the marketplace with all of the different plans available. That is why it is so important for you to first have your goals established.

Concentrate on an area of investing. This means you focus, at least in the beginning, both in one geographic area as well as with one type of property. It's possible that as you get comfortable with your investments and gain experience in what works (and what doesn't), you may want to move on to other areas of investments.

The authors of this book invest primarily in two different areas: large apartment buildings and working-class three-bedroom, two-bathroom homes. Other successful investors invest only in commercial properties. The right real estate investment for your plan depends on your goals, skills, and interests. The best way to find the best plan is to learn more about each type of investment.

Diane's Personal Plan—An Example of a Plan

I have almost always worked as an S (self-employed person) in my CPA profession. *Cashflow Quadrant,* by Robert Kiyosaki and Sharon Lechter, explains further the definition and characteristics of an S as well as discussing the other three income-producing methods in our economy: as an E (employee), B (business owner), and I (investor). My goal was to build cash flow that showed up every month. I wanted a high return and didn't want the hassle of being a landlord. Based on those needs, my husband, Richard, and I invested as a Rent to Buy landlord. This rental program allowed us to receive passive income without many of the typical landlord hassles.

Under the Rent to Buy program tenants pay an option down and a portion of each month's rent goes toward the ultimate purchase of the home. They have a period of two to three years, depending on the contract, in which to exercise the option. If they don't exercise the option in that time, we agree to renegotiate the contract provided the property is in good condition and all payments have been made on time.

There are many advantages to us with this program, including: (1) higher cash flow (people will pay more knowing that they have a possibility of owning the property), (2) tenants are responsible for all repairs, and (3) tenants are motivated to make all payments in a timely manner.

We look for properties in working-class neighborhoods using the pickup truck factor. (We look for neighborhoods where there are more pickup trucks than passenger cars. If they have writing on the side like "Smith Construction" or "Ernie's Plumbing" – so much the better.) We then look for properties that are a little distressed but with no structural problems. Our goal is to buy them at 80 percent of market value and then renovate only the items that will bring the most return, based on a buyer's perceived value of the change.

We then "sell" the homes under the Rent to Buy program using an ad designed to bring in people with credit problems who still want to own their own home. We show the houses at open houses only (no appointments) and hire others to sit the open houses. Richard closes the deal with a 3 percent to 5 percent option down (nonrefundable) and a payment based on the assumed appreciation price of the home in two to three years. The tenants then pay us rent with a portion going toward the future purchase price.

At the expiration of the option period, they either buy the home from us (using their initial option money plus the amount accrued from each monthly payment as the down payment) or, if all payments have been on time and the property is in good condition, we will agree to renegotiate.

Our return on this program averages 20 to 50 percent cash-on-cash return. The tenants are responsible for all repairs and we take full advantage of the tax advantages of real estate investing until they buy the property from us.

This investment plan works well for us because while we have the money to invest in buying the properties (typically 10 percent down), we don't have much time to invest.

After following this program for over seven years, we have found that few ever buy us out. Instead, the tenants either leave (forfeiting their deposits) or renegotiate (i.e., increase) the purchase price and cash flow to us. During this time, we've received cash flow and the properties have gone up in value. In the past six months, we have received, tax free, over $100,000 from refinancing these properties. This money was reinvested, so that it all continues to grow.

For more information regarding the Rent to Buy program, see www.taxloopholes.com.

Becoming a Large Real Estate Investor

There is a barrier for many investors that occurs at four or five properties. The investor can't seem to move beyond that level of ownership. Typically, a seminar room full of experienced real estate investors will only have about 10 percent that own more than five properties. The reason for this barrier is that the complexity goes up as the number of properties increases. Many systems and team members can only handle a small volume. If you want to increase the volume, you will need to tighten your systems and your team members will need to tighten theirs as well.

One of the key distinctions between the small and large real estate investor has to do with their bookkeeping tasks. A small investor can easily handle the record-keeping requirements for just a few properties. But, if you want to grow your business, you will need to have professional help in this area.

Real Estate Accounting Needs

There are specific issues related to bookkeeping for real estate investors. Unfortunately, real estate bookkeeping is more complicated than bookkeeping for your small business. Part of that complexity is due to the many different programs available for real estate investment. Each program has its own peculiarities.

The workbook *Easy Accounting for Real Estate Investors*, by Diane Kennedy and available at www.taxloopholes.com, discusses the specific accounting to use for many of the different real estate investing plans. Make sure your tax strategist, bookkeeper, and other members of your team understand the accounting and tax issues for your investment plan. Here are a few topics to consider:

BUY AND QUICK FLIP

* *Advantages*: You will make money for more investments.
* *Disadvantages*: You may have to hold the property for an extended period, longer than you intended. If you don't have a contingency plan with how to hold, and pay for, the property, you could go broke. If you are successful at selling the property in a short time, the income earned from the flip will be taxed at ordinary tax rates.
* *Bookkeeping Issues*: Make sure you count all expenses in the flip process. This type of property, which moves on and off the records quickly, is prone to bad record keeping. Often the owner doesn't keep it long enough to have a good system.

HOLD FOR LONG-TERM APPRECIATION

* *Advantages*: You have been able to take advantage of leverage to build your own net worth. The gain will be subject to the lower capital gains rate. Or, if you have invested in your principal residence, after two years any gain up to $500,000 will be tax-free ($250,000 if you are single).

- *Disadvantages*: You may have to carry the property out of other sources of income.
- *Bookkeeping Issues*: Since this is a long-term hold, you will need to keep records for as long as you have the property.

RENTAL, ANTICIPATED TO HOLD LONG TERM

- *Advantages*: Cash flow! Someone else is building your net worth, paying off your debt, and providing you with passive income.
- *Disadvantages*: Along with this come the responsibilities of being a landlord. In some cases, cash flow properties don't go up in value as quickly.
- *Bookkeeping Issues*: See Chapter 9 for ideas on how to accelerate depreciation. In some cases, the paper loss of real estate cannot offset other income. See Chapter 10 to learn about the loophole of qualifying as a real estate professional so you can offset other income with this paper loss.

LAND DEVELOPMENT

- *Advantages*: Done right, you can make a lot of money.
- *Disadvantages*: This is truly a business. You will need to consider financing, development, marketing, and the associated risks. Meanwhile, you don't have a tenant helping you make the payments.
- *Bookkeeping Issues*: Development costs must be capitalized, not expensed. This means that you are paying a lot of money for development and not able to take a current deduction for it. If you are a land developer, you may also run into a tax problem called uniform capitalization. This means that you will be required to capitalize normal operating expenses in addition to the development costs.

SELL ON RENT TO BUY PROGRAM

- *Advantages*: Cash flow without the headaches of management!
- *Disadvantages*: You must make sure the program is set up correctly, or you won't have the benefits of ownership during the time you hold the property. If you have created a sale at the beginning of the transaction, you may be forced to recognize gain initially, without yet receiving the money. You also may give up some of the potential appreciation if your tenants exercise their option.
- *Bookkeeping Issues*: Since the tenants will pay a portion of the impound account property tax and insurance, you will need to have

accurate accounting of these items. Make sure an attorney reviews your contracts.

FIX UP AND SELL

- *Advantages*: Profit!
- *Disadvantages*: You will either need to do the work, or find someone else to do it. You have also potentially created a job for yourself. The gain will be taxed at an ordinary tax rate if you hold the property for less than one year. Also remember, you will need to pay for the repair costs or arrange for a construction loan.
- *Bookkeeping Issues*: Make sure you keep good track of the expenses involved in the fix-up process.

FIX UP AND HOLD

- *Advantages*: Enhanced cash flow!
- *Disadvantages*: Same as with fix up and sell, you have potentially created a job for yourself.
- *Bookkeeping Issues*: You might be forced to capitalize the repair work. In some cases, tax credits are available for pre-1936 buildings, historically designated properties, and repairs done to facilitate ADA (disability) needs.

What's Next?

Just as with any improvement plan, you need to reassess your financial standing after a few months from the purchase of your investment. It typically takes up to six months to adequately settle a new property with the optimal tenants and management. Look at what worked and what didn't. It's a useful exercise that helps you refine your plan.

Some of the most winning stories have come from people who reassess their progress on a monthly or even weekly basis. As well, your progress can be shaped and enhanced through continuing education. You should consider utilizing seminars, tapes, and books to improve your understanding. The SuccessDNA *Guide to Real Estate Investment and Management,* available at www.successdna.com, is a good overview book. There are many others. Reading, attending seminars, and learning and thinking about real estate, as you are now, will improve both your intellect and your return on investment.

Part Two

Tax Secrets

Chapter Four

Introduction to Tax Secrets

Why Can't I Ever Get a Straight Answer on a Tax Question?

Have you ever wondered why you can't get a straight answer to your tax questions? Or worse, have you asked numerous people and gotten numerous answers? Why does this happen? The answer is quite simple. It happens because tax law is complex.

There are over 500,000 pages of written tax law. And, what's more, it is constantly changing and being modified. Every day is a new day when it comes to taxes! Consider that there were over 400 IRS Code changes for 2001. For every Code change, there are one to five Treasury Regulations, Revenue Rulings, Revenue Procedures, and eventually multiple Tax Court cases. Over 400 Code changes occurred in 2001, which was considered pretty uneventful when it came to tax changes.

Now let's add another layer of complexity. There are three different key players in determining tax law: Congress (which frequently changes), the IRS, and multiple Tax Court districts. Sometimes these different players don't agree. There are numerous instances of conflicting Tax Court opinions. Sometimes the code is not even consistent within itself.

To make it even more complicated, tax law is comprised of both facts and opinions. A fact is something that can be proven to exist via physical evidence, and an opinion is something that may or may not be true. A tax fact is clear-cut, such as what line you put income on. A tax opinion is how much income needs to go on that line. Most tax decisions are made based on opinion. Fortunately, there is a lot of guidance in tax law that helps informed and educated tax strategists make good decisions. The problem occurs when partially informed people try to make tax decisions. It is a full-time job tracking all of the law changes. This is something that the casual advisor cannot do well.

The worst answers of all can come directly from the IRS. IRS agents are only given three days training before they are let loose on the service center telephones as "experts." IRS agents frequently don't even have accounting degrees. And, if you get bad advice, the IRS is not liable for giving you that bad advice.

Of course, your own circumstances will be unique to you. That is when you need to rely on your tax experts to further interpret the entire body of tax law based on what you want and need. It's not your job to be the tax expert (unless, of course, that really is your job). It is, however, your role to understand what they are talking about.

Three-Stage Tax Formula

But how can you become an expert on over 500,000 pages of constantly changing tax law? You can't. But there *is* a simple formula that explains how tax in the U.S. is calculated. Called the Three-Stage Tax Formula, it can be found in *Loopholes of the Rich,* by Diane Kennedy.

There are three different stages to the calculation of income tax:

- First you report *income*.
- From income you subtract *deductible expenses* to come to the amount of taxable income.
- The taxable income is then multiplied by the *tax rate* to determine the amount of tax.

A good tax strategy will encompass each of these stages. The key is to learn how you can manipulate to your advantage, using IRS-approved loopholes, each of these stages.

- *Income*: What is income? What are the different types of income? How can you change from one type of income to another and why does it matter? How can you turn taxable income into tax-deferred income or tax-free income?

- *Deductible Expenses*: What expenses are deductible? How can you make use of multiple business structures to create expenses on one side that are not income on the other? What personal expenses do you have now that are really hidden business deductions?

- *Tax Rate*: One of the best provisions that we in the U.S. have that other countries do not, is the ability to make use of a graduated tax rate. This means that there is not a flat rate applied to your taxable income. Instead, a portion of your income is taxed at one rate and then the next layer of income is taxed at a higher rate, and so on. If, for example, you have a tax rate of 28 percent for your personal return, this means that you have filled the portion allowed at ten percent and 15 percent, and for every additional dollar you make, you will pay 28 percent. You do not pay 28 percent on all of the income, just that final portion. We call 28 percent your marginal tax rate. How can you move income from your higher tax rate to a lower (or zero) tax rate?

A financial and tax strategy that incorporates real estate is the easiest way to positively affect *all* levels of the three stages—income, expenses, and tax rate. Real estate also allows an employee to deduct many business expenses that normally would not be deducted against their wages. Finally, real estate, more than any other type of investment, has the widest range of tax law available to reduce, and even eliminate, tax.

In the next three chapters, we will go through each stage and see how real estate can affect income.

Chapter 5

Three Types of Income

Three Baskets of Income Defined

Since the 1986 Tax Reform Act, the IRS has defined three different baskets of income. These are:

- Earned income: You work for the money.
- Passive income: Your business or real estate works for you.
- Portfolio income: Your money works for you.

Earned income is taxed at the ordinary tax rate, plus if you have the wrong business structure in place, you will also pay the self-employment tax of 15.3 percent. If you paid at the highest tax rate in 2002, that would mean a tax rate of over 53 percent, for federal tax alone!

Most portfolio income is in the form of capital gains, which has a maximum rate of 18 percent or 20 percent, depending on how long the asset has been held.

Passive income that is earned from real estate, if set up correctly, can receive cash flow with no tax whatsoever. See Chapter 9, "Loophole #2: Accelerating Depreciation," for ideas on how to do that.

Just based on tax rates alone, it makes sense to move from earned income to portfolio or passive income. Real estate investing can help you do that.

One important note about the three baskets of income: There are many restrictions on losses and expenses that are incurred within these three categories. For example, you are limited in the amount of passive loss that you can take against earned income. You are similarly limited in the amount of portfolio loss (such as investment expenses or loss on sale of stock) that you can take against earned income.

Real Estate Losses

Since 1986, U.S. tax laws have stated that losses can only be claimed against income in the same category. For example, passive losses can only be used against other passive income. You cannot take passive losses against earned income. Investment expenses, such as for margin interest or investment education, can only go against portfolio income.

In the case of real estate, the rules regarding passive losses are more complicated. If your income is less than $100,000, you are allowed up to $25,000 in losses from your real estate against other income. If you have more than $25,000 in losses, the excess amount is held as what is called an unallowed loss until a future date when you sell the property. You don't lose the loss, but it's not very good tax planning to put off that loss to the future.

If your income is $100,000 or more, the amount of loss you can currently deduct is phased out. The unallowed loss is suspended against a future date when you sell the property. So, the loss isn't lost, but it is deferred. That's not great planning either!

Here's the loophole: Qualify as a real estate professional. If you are a real estate professional, you have unlimited losses possible. More on how to do that in Chapter 10.

Taxable Income

The three baskets of income are considered taxable income, although passive income may be taxable with no tax assigned. The IRS defines taxable income as gross income and says that "Except as otherwise provided . . . gross income means all income from whatever source derived." The best tax planning is in finding the loopholes that are defined within the "except as otherwise provided" wording.

Another of the great loopholes available through real estate is the ability to take money out of a property as "otherwise provided." In other words, you can take money out of a property and it will not be considered taxable income.

Appreciation

Property has always gone up in value, if you look at it with the long-term perspective. Now, this does not mean that property will *always* go up, especially if you take a short-term (less than five-year) view. And, of course, if someone pays too much for property it may take a very long time to see it go up to that value (and perhaps not in one's lifetime). But, when you do have appreciation, you can take advantage of that appreciation by taking the money out tax-free through loans.

Tax-Advantaged Income

The IRS has provided ways to take what would otherwise be taxable income and turn it into tax-deferred or tax-free income. Tax-deferred income means that you put off having to pay tax until a later date. The benefit is that your money grows at a faster pace. For example, assume you pay tax at a 28 percent marginal tax rate and you invest $1,000 per year. After taking out for taxes, you actually have only $720 available for future investment. On the other hand, if all of the amount can continue to grow, there is more available to grow. For example, if you invest $1,000 per year at 12 percent for twenty years, the difference between paying tax each year and being able to defer the tax to a future date would mean an additional $6,456 in wealth. If you invest for ten years, the difference is only $1,179. The unknown factors, of course, include the amount of interest you will earn and the future tax rate.

Tax-free income, on the other hand, means that not only does the investment grow without tax, but you can also liquidate that investment and take the value without paying tax on it. Obviously, tax-free income is the best way, wherever possible.

Tax-Deferred Income

There are two primary ways to turn otherwise taxable income into tax-deferred income. One is through a business structure or business entity that allows you to have tax-deferred income. A pension plan is an example of a business structure that allows you to defer tax.

The second way is through specific Code provisions allowed for certain types of investments. Currently, under U.S. tax law, you can exchange, in certain circumstances, to defer the gain on real estate. The most common way an exchange is done is through what is known variously as a like-kind exchange, a Starker exchange, or a Section 1031 exchange. These are all different ways of saying the same thing.

The like-kind exchange is described in IRC Section 1031 and further defined in a court ruling, *Starker v. Commissioner*—hence the other names. This is a specific exchange of real estate that has been held for business or investment. You cannot do a like-kind exchange (under this Code section) on your personal residence or on non–real estate items. The like-kind exchange allows you to sell a piece of property that is highly appreciated and roll over the gain into another piece of property. The second piece of property merely has to be another piece of business or investment real estate. It does not need to be the same type of investment property. You can exchange from many properties into one property or vice versa. For example, you could exchange a single-family residence into an apartment building or a single-family residence into many single-family residences or bare land into two single-family residences. . . . the possibilities are almost endless.

There are some rules for a like-kind exchange that must be closely followed. See Chapter 11, "Loophole #4: Sell Now, Tax Later," for more details. If you are considering a like-kind exchange, make sure you notify the real estate agent who is selling your property, as well as the title company. They will put you in touch with an exchange agent who will facilitate the sale.

Tax-Free Income

Tax-deferred income means that you will pay tax at a future date on the income. Tax-free income means that you *never* pay tax on that income. Obviously, tax-free income is the way to go!

Much as with tax-deferred income, there are two ways that you can have tax-free income. The first way is through the type of business or investment structure such as a Roth IRA.

The second way to produce tax-free income is through specific provisions within the current tax law as they pertain to real estate. The best example of that currently is with the tax-free gain that is allowed through the sale of your principal residence. You can now deduct $250,000 (if you are single) of gain on the sale of a home you have lived in for two of the past five years. If you are married, the exclusion amount jumps to $500,000. Chapter 8,

"Loophole #1: Principal Residence," will go over in greater detail how you can make use of this tax gift from Congress. Don't miss out on this exclusion!

Why Type of Income Matters

Once you understand what *is* taxable income (versus tax-free cash receipt, tax-deferred, or tax-free growth) and what *type* of income you have, you might find that you want to change the character of the income you have.

Earned income means just that—you have to earn it. If your goal is truly financial freedom, which means that money you don't work for (passive and portfolio) exceeds your monthly expenses, then you want to turn earned income into the other forms. You can do that with your business, particularly if it is in the form of a C corporation. If you currently have a business producing income, you may want to discover the ways to change the type of income from your business (earned) into passive through the use of real estate.

You can learn how to change the character of the income you make through your business from earned to passive: This can be done through the use of a C corporation. The C corporation is a type of business structure that has unique properties. Some of these properties are discussed in greater detail in the Rich Dad's Advisors books, *Loopholes of the Rich: How the Rich Legally Make More Money and Pay Less Tax* and *Own Your Own Corporation.*

"It's not how MUCH money you make. It's the TYPE of money you make that determines whether you can take advantage of legal loopholes."

Chapter 6

Legal Deductions

Business Setup

Real estate can be set up in a number of different types of structures. Regardless of which type of structure you use—regular Schedule E attachment to your individual income tax return, partnership, and so on—the activities can be considered as a business. This means that in addition to the special tax loopholes available from real estate you also can take advantage of the deductions available from owning your own business.

The income from real estate can be of different types—property management fees, real estate commissions, gain from sale, passive income flow from rent, or portfolio income (interest) from real estate mortgages. The type of deduction can be limited based on the type of income.

Chapter 21 will discuss the different business structures possible for real estate. Plus, be sure to review Chapter 20 to review the asset protection and potential liability issues important for your real estate holdings.

Real Estate Is a Business

One unexpected benefit from investing in real estate is that for many people this will be the only business they are able to have. Our tax code has been set up to benefit business owners and, in some cases, self-employed persons. The difference between a business owner and a self-employed person is that a self-employed person needs to show up every day in order to have an income. A business owner is able to work *on* his business and not *in* his business. But both have tax advantages over the regular W-2 wage earner. There are very few tax deductions available for the W-2 wage earner and, even worse, as their income rises, they begin to lose both tax deductions and tax exemptions. They are severely penalized for making more income and also do not have the benefit of the business owner's write-offs.

Yet for many people with family responsibilities and financial commitments, there is little hope that they will ever be able to leave the eight-to-five job without endangering their family's financial situation. But they can begin a real estate investment program, part-time, after work and on their own terms. As shown in *Real Estate Riches: How to Become Rich Using Your Banker's Money* by Dolf de Roos, real estate is the way for anyone to add to their wealth and increase their cash flow so that they have a financial hope for the future.

It is also a business. That means that there are deductions against the real estate income that are possible for wage earners who have never before had that possibility. Learning what to deduct is a whole new mind-set and can feel confusing to the first-time business owner.

This book has been written especially to help the first-time real estate investor in discovering the best tax strategies for their new business. Besides the special rules for real estate, there are also the basic deductions available for real estate that any business can have.

Hidden Business Deductions

What's deductible? If you are asking that question, you're like most of the clients we talk to at DKA. And, the answer is (again!): "It depends." You see, the IRS is purposely vague in what can be deducted in your business. That is because everyone's circumstances are different.

The only guidance we get from the IRS on business deductions is just twenty-seven words. There are some exceptions to this brief definition, but basically, if you follow this guideline, you'll do fine.

TWENTY-SEVEN WORDS
The IRS defines, in just twenty-seven words, at Internal Revenue Code Section 162(a), what is deductible:

There shall be allowed as a deduction, all the ordinary and necessary expenses paid or incurred during the taxable year in carrying on any trade or business.

Now, here's the challenge: Who defines what is "ordinary" and what is "necessary"?

In fact, it's all subject to interpretation, like a lot of the Tax Code. Congress writes a tax act, which is followed by the Tax Code. After the new Code comes out, the IRS eventually writes Treasury Regulations, which serve to explain how the Code is applied. And then, added to that, are the numerous IRS publications, Revenue Rulings, Revenue Procedures, and Tax Court decisions that further explain and interpret the Code. And when it comes to defining "ordinary" and "necessary," there have been a lot of federal court decisions trying to interpret what those words mean. The most consistent explanations have been:

- *Ordinary Expenses:* Expenses that are normal, common, and accepted under the circumstances by the business community.
- *Necessary Expenses:* Expenses that are appropriate and helpful.

Go to the DKA Web page at www.dkacpa.com for the "Where Does Your Money Go?" questionnaire. You can download this form free. Using that, consider where your money goes. Which one of your expenses could be considered ordinary and necessary to your real estate business?

Where Does Your Money Go?

Deductions reduce your taxable income. That means that your overall tax is less. Yet the sad fact is that these deductions are only available to business owners. In other words, if you're an employee, you're out of luck. Your boss (the business owner) gets the deductions. One of the benefits of real estate investing is that you can keep your day job (as an employee) and still get to take legal deductions against your real estate income stream.

Why look for deductions? It's simple—the more tax deductions your business can take, the lower your taxable income is. The form "Where Does Your Money Go?" was developed to identify what deductions you might already have and find ways to legitimately write off future expenses that are planned.

To get you started, here are some of the most commonly overlooked business deductions. Chances are you have these deductions available already for your business.

Most Commonly Missed Deductions for Real Estate

Following are the business deductions common to almost all businesses. Take the time to review the list and make a note of ones that might be applicable to your business.

AUTO EXPENSE

There are many ways to deduct the cost of an auto. And that can be confusing. Using the values for the year 2002, here are the simple facts about autos.

You can buy the car in your real estate business. The business can deduct the cost of maintaining the car (gas, oil, repairs, tires, car washes, and other expenses). Plus, the business can deduct the interest portion of any payments and then depreciate the car, using the limits established by the government. There are limitations on the amount of depreciation per year you can take for passenger automobiles. A passenger automobile is any four-wheeled vehicle manufactured primarily for use on public streets with an unloaded gross vehicle weight (GVW) of 6,000 pounds or less. A truck or van is treated as a passenger automobile if it has a GVW of 6,000 or less. Vehicles with GVW of greater than 6,000 are not subject to these limits.

Your business can lease the car. Passenger vehicles will have a small portion that will be deductible. See your tax consultant for exactly how much you can deduct.

You can buy or lease the car yourself, and be reimbursed for mileage at the current rate. In 2003, the amount is $0.36 per mile. The payment is deducted from the business income, but is not considered income for you.

Make the IRS happy: Keep track of your mileage for appointments. A handy way to do that is in your PDA (personal digital assistant) or daily scheduler. Make a record of all appointments and, if your record is kept in an electronic scheduler, make sure you keep a backup on your computer. Include trips to the bank, mortgage brokers, real estate subdivision—wherever you might go for business.

> The following deduction for a heavy vehicle is not available for real estate investments that have solely passive income. Only a company that generates earned income can take the Section 179 deduction.

If you buy a vehicle that is over 6,000 GVW, the standard automobile limitation does not apply. In this case, your business can depreciate the vehicle just as if it were any other item of equipment. That includes being able to make a Section 179 deduction of $24,000 (in 2002) right up front.

BUSINESS START-UP

There are many expenses *before* you begin your real estate investing business. One of those costs is likely to be your accounting system, software, and computer. And, unfortunately, since one of the steps is setting up your accounting system, and the expenses occur first, you might forget them.

> Remember to include the cost of equipment and furniture for your home office that you contribute to your business as business expenses.

Here is a checklist of common start-up expenses that you can deduct (or capitalize and deduct over sixty months). Please note that it is not complete. Use it as a memory jog for items you can deduct in your business.

• *Legal expenses* (will need to be amortized over sixty months): These are costs that you pay to an attorney or document preparation service to prepare the initial paperwork for your business. These need to be amortized over sixty months. In other words, you can subtract one sixtieth of the cost each month. After the business is going, most legal fees are deductible immediately.

• *Business structure setup* (amortized over sixty months): This includes the costs you pay to have special business structures set up—such as the cost of forming a limited liability company (LLC).

• *Filing fees*: These are the costs paid to the state and local agencies for the privilege of doing business and include business licenses, state filing fees,

fees for lists of directors, and others. The exact fees will depend on the type and location of your business.

• *Accounting fees*: Hopefully, you will consult with an accountant and bookkeeper to get your books set up as soon as possible. Those costs are deductible.

• *Office equipment*. There is a lot of equipment needed for a basic office in this electronic age. Computer, printer, fax machine, phone—these are just a few of the items needed. Many people already have some of these items before starting a business. Your business can pay you the fair market value for these items from its proceeds, but you need to track the expenses first.

• *Office furniture*: Office furniture can include your desk, tables, chairs, and filing cabinets, as well as art you hang on the walls. These costs will be depreciated over five to seven years.

• *Cost of investigating business* (seminars, books, travel, advisors' fees): A prudent business owner takes time to investigate and learn all they can about their business first. This can include going to seminars, buying books, subscribing to magazines, dues paid to professional organizations, and travel to look at other businesses and talk to advisors. And, especially, in the case of a real estate investor—it involves looking at real estate. And, real estate is everywhere!

• *Office setup costs* (stationery, business cards, logo design): The cost of designing a logo, setting up a Web site, preparing stationery, and so on are all part of the office setup costs.

Make the IRS happy! To make sure there is no problem down the line with the start-up expenses, keep good records. If you have paid for items before your business is really set up (as is frequently the case), create an expense reimbursement form.

MEALS AND ENTERTAINMENT

The most common mistake for beginning business owners is to fail to count their business and entertaining expenses. *Any* expense that is "directly related" to the business or "associated with" the business, and business is discussed, and the entertainment takes place immediately before or after a business decision, is deductible. Currently, 50 percent of the cost is deductible.

Make the IRS happy! For each meal expense, keep a copy of the meal receipt and record (1) who you had the meal with, (2) what you discussed, and (3) when it occurred.

TRAVEL EXPENSES

One huge benefit of having your own real estate investing operating as a business is that, with the right documentation, you can write it all off.

Prove that you had a business purpose to your trip by keeping business cards of real estate agents and property developments, folders, promotional materials, anything that proves that the trip helped your business.

On a trip, if you have more business days (a day in which you perform business activities) than nonbusiness days, then the cost of the travel is deductible.

WRITE OFF YOUR KIDS!

There are many expenses associated with your children. The best plan is to have your children employed in your business so that they can pay for their own expenses. In this way, you are able to deduct the cost of their salary, and up to $4,700 is not taxable to them (in 2002). There are numerous tasks that you can have your children do in your real estate business—mowing lawns, cleanup in your home office, basic filing, cleanup of new properties, and much else.

Keep the IRS happy! To legally pay your children, make sure you follow these three simple rules:

- Have a written job description;
- Have your child keep track of their hours, just like any other employee would; and
- Pay a reasonable wage for the work performed.

Rich Dad Tip

Pay your child a salary so that they can begin to build their own pension fund. Once they have earned income, they can legally have a Roth IRA account, which will grow tax-free for them.

HOME OFFICE EXPENSE

Many people seem to be afraid of the home office expense. That fear is unfounded, even though it persists. Perhaps it is because this deduction has gone through some wild swings in the last decade. Currently, a home office is allowed for a self-employed person or a flow-through entity as long as the space has exclusive business purpose and you have a business. In other words, the home office must be in a room that is only used for a business purpose. To calculate the home office expense, follow these steps:

Square footage of the room used for the business	A	_____
Square footage of the entire home	B	_____
Business percentage (divide A by B)		_____%

The business percentage is then applied against your home costs, such as:

- Mortgage interest
- Property tax
- Rent
- Homeowner's association dues
- Home maintenance costs
- Janitorial expenses
- Utilities (gas, electric, water, garbage, etc.)
- Insurance
- Private mortgage insurance

The business percentage times these expenses is then used to directly offset the business income.

Keep the IRS happy! You will want to be able to prove exclusive business purpose. We recommend to our clients that they take a picture of their office and sketch a basic floor plan that shows the room in relationship to other rooms, with square footage indicated. That way, you have proof of the business purpose of the space, even after you have sold the home.

PHANTOM EXPENSE

One of the biggest benefits for real estate is the phantom expense of depreciation. We call it a phantom expense because it is a deduction that you don't have to pay for. In other words, you could buy a property with no money down and still be able to take a deduction for depreciation. This is one of the loopholes that prove that the IRS supports ownership of real estate.

You see, while historically property goes up in value, the government allows you to take a deduction for the depreciation, which assumes that it goes down in value. This phantom expense allows you to receive cash flow from your investment property and yet pay little or no tax on the income. It's the best deal going.

Remember that only real property, not land, is depreciable. If you are a developer, many real costs are not deductible in the current year—this is a trap for the unwary.

If you buy a piece of property to improve or change such as by subdivision, you are considered a developer. The income that you earn on this project is considered business or trade income, which means that earnings would be subject to self-employment tax like any other earned income. Additionally, costs to improve the property and holding costs (mortgage interest and property tax) must be capitalized. This means that those costs are added to the basis of the property and deducted against the income from the sale. Basis starts with either the purchase price of the property or the basis from a prior property that has been rolled into the purchase during a like-kind exchange. Items such as capital improvements, recording fees, title search, and the like increase basis. It is decreased by depreciation, easements, and so forth. Chapter 11, "Loophole #4: Sell Now, Tax Later," discusses basis calculation and like-kind exchanges in more detail. You will spend current dollars for a future deduction.

Additionally, developers (just like any other form of manufacturers) are subject to the Uniform Capitalization rules (also known as Section 263A). Under these rules, you must capitalize a percentage of all general and administrative costs. The percentage that must be capitalized is based on a calculation of inventory that you hold versus inventory that has been sold. The rules are complicated in both determining what items of expense are subject to Section 263A and in calculating the formula. Make sure that your Tax Advisor is fully aware of the complexity of Uniform Capitalization if you are a developer.

Special Deduction Rules for Real Estate Investment

Real estate has a few special rules regarding deductions. Following are some of them:

Costs that go into creating an asset—such as construction—are capitalized and depreciated. That means that what you pay money for now might not be deductible now. Look for ways to deduct expenses instead of being forced to capitalize them by separating out repair expenses from capitalizable improvements.

Real estate investing is not allowed a Section 179 deduction. That means that you cannot take this expense deduction for personal property directly associated with your real property. Instead, it must be capitalized and then depreciated. However, the personal property component of your property can use the Section 179 deduction. See Chapter 9, "Loophole #2: Accelerating Depreciation," for ways to determine the personal property amount.

One benefit that real estate has is the ability to leverage depreciation. In other words, if you buy a property with only 10 percent down, you can still depreciate the real property that is financed. You are able to leverage both appreciation and depreciation with real estate.

The ability to accelerate depreciation will be covered in greater detail in Chapter 9.

Chapter 7

Tax Rate Magic

The third element in a good tax strategy is controlling the tax rate. In real estate, there are even more opportunities to take advantage of lower tax rates due to special loopholes written for real estate and special capital gains treatment.

No Tax

First of all, consider maximizing your principal residence gain exclusion. It's tax-free money! See Chapter 8, "Loophole #1: Principal Residence," for some techniques to making sure you always get this deduction.

The type of entity you use could also mean you have no tax. See Chapter 13, "Loophole #6: Real Estate Investing with Your Pension Plan," for ideas on how to buy real estate with your pension fund. If you use a Roth IRA, that could mean no tax, ever.

Deferred Tax

There are three ways to hold or transact real estate in a way that tax can be deferred. Sometimes you can defer that tax forever!

INSTALLMENT SALE

If you sell a property over time, that is called an installment sale. In other words, you will receive separate payments over time. Each payment you receive is composed of at least two parts: (1) principal and (2) interest. The interest received will always be taxable just like any other portfolio income. However, in the case of the principal, it will actually only be partially taxable, depending on how it is apportioned between gain and return of capital.

The calculation is important for two reasons: (1) You are required to report the mortgage interest that you receive on a Form 1098 on an annual basis to the person paying you. (2) You will need that calculation for completion of your year-end tax return. In both cases, I strongly recommend that you use a qualified accountant to prepare and calculate the forms (or at least to check your math!).

There is one word of warning regarding installment sales. If you are considered a dealer (involved in the trade or business of real estate trading), you can not qualify for installment sale treatment on payments. If you are a dealer, you must take all of the gain as taxable immediately. That means you could be in the position of paying tax on income you have not yet received.

The IRS defines a dealer disposition (in other words, a transaction by a dealer) as "(1) any disposition of personal property by a person who regularly sells or otherwise disposes of such property of the installment plan and (2) any disposition of real property that is held by the taxpayer for sale to customers in the ordinary course of the taxpayer's trade or business." In other words, if you are involved in real estate investing (and thus a trade or business), you are probably a dealer.

Warning

There is a fallacy promoted by some non–tax professionals that a person can avoid the dealer status issue by forming a business structure to sell the property. If the actions of a person create a dealer situation, then a business acting in the same way will create a dealer situation as well. The key is to always have qualified advisors on your team who are accountable for the advice they give.

BUYING REAL ESTATE THROUGH YOUR PENSION PLAN

With a regular pension plan, the gain is deferred until you withdraw it from your pension plan. With a Roth plan, you never pay tax. For more on this, see Chapter 13.

SECTION 1031 LIKE-KIND EXCHANGE

Also known as Starker exchange, under these provisions you can roll your property into another property and defer the tax to a future date. There are specific requirements on the 1031 exchange, which are covered in more depth in Chapter 11.

Capital Gains

When a property sells, the calculation for gain is comprised of two parts:

1. *Recapture of previously taken depreciation:* The first step to the calculation of tax due when a property sells is to recapture or add back all the depreciation previously expensed. The snag is that you may be required to recapture depreciation you haven't even taken. The IRS Code requires you to recapture all depreciation that was previously allowed or allowable. This recaptured depreciation is then taxed at ordinary tax rates.

Warning

Occasionally, I hear reports of taxpayers not taking the depreciation on their investment property because they have been told they would just have to "pay tax on it later" when it sells. This is bad advice! You will have to add back the depreciation, whether you took the deduction or not!

Solution:

If you have not previously taken depreciation on an investment property you currently hold, the IRS will allow you to catch up by filing Form 3115 with your tax return. We also recommend that you attach a statement to your return, explaining the catch-up depreciation in the current year.

---

2. *Capital gains rate applied to gain (after recapture of depreciation):*
The capital gains tax rate is determined based on the holding period of the property. If the property is held less than twelve months, then the ordinary tax rate would apply. If the property is held twelve months or longer, but less than five years, the maximum tax rate is 20 percent. Effective after December 31, 2000, the maximum capital gains rate of 18 percent is applied if the asset is held for five or more years. For individuals in the 10 percent or 15 percent tax bracket, the maximum capital gains rate is 8 percent.

The rules are a little confusing as to when this new rule is effective. If the taxpayer is in the tax bracket that is higher than 15 percent, the five-year holding period rule is only applicable for assets acquired after December 31, 2000. If the individual is in the 10 percent or 15 percent tax bracket, the asset does not have to be acquired after December 31, 2000, in order to qualify for the 8 percent rate. In other words, individuals in the lower tax brackets may already be able to take advantage of the new lower capital gains rate.

Chapter 8

Loophole #1:
Principal Residence

In the next seven chapters, we're going to cover seven of the over 100 loopholes available for real estate investors and real estate investors who operate as a business. For information on even more loopholes go to www.taxloop holes.com for tax strategies and free tax tips.

No Visible Means of Support—Diane's Story

The wake-up call for this huge tax benefit came to me when I received a call from my mortgage broker, Alec. Alec was requesting a stated income for a mutual client, John. John was one of my real estate heroes. He was single, lived well, and not only did he not have to pay taxes, he generally didn't even have to file a tax return. And he did it all perfectly legally!

During that phone call, Alec told me about the new deal John had found. But first we discussed the great deal he had just completed. Two years prior he had bought a major fixer-upper home for $65,000 in a neighborhood that was quickly on its way up. This house represented too much work for people like me who looked for quick little fixes that created appreciation.

This home took about $50,000 in material costs to renovate. He lived in the house while he did the work and contributed his labor to the project. John had a real talent for general construction as well as the details of restoration. During that time, the house was his only job . . . and it was a very part-time job at that.

At the end of two years, he sold the property for $250,000. That meant a gain for him of $135,000 in two years. And that gain was completely tax-free. If he had worked at a job, he would have had to make over $200,000 to get that same amount. He did it, part-time.

John could actually have received up to $250,000 in tax-free gain because this was his principal residence and he had lived in it for two of the previous five years.

The part that got to me, though, was that during his free time he had found his next deal. And it was right under my nose. As I listened to Alec during this phone call, I realized it was the small office building with four units behind it that I drove by every day but had been too busy to notice. John not only noticed the property but acted. The property needed some work and the elderly owner (who lived in one of the units) was anxious to move. Unfortunately for him, no one was interested in the property because of the work needed on the back units. So John waited until the property had been on the market for a while and then made the owner an offer. He found 90 percent financing through Alec and the owner agreed to carry back a note for the rest. With the money John would make on his house sale, he'd be able to live and do the mainly cosmetic repairs that were needed. The property would cash-flow immediately to him from the tenants already in place. Once the repairs were done, he could increase the rents and make even more. And he did it all without any of his own money!

"How did we miss that deal, Alec?" I asked during the call, a little jealously. Alec and I had offices on the same street and took the same path to work each day. Here was a great deal we drove by every day and we both missed it.

"John doesn't work. That's the secret—you and I were too busy with our businesses to notice what was right under our noses," Alec explained.

Alec was right—we missed the deal because we were too busy. John supported himself by finding fixer-upper houses in up-and-coming neighborhoods. He moved in and did the fix-up work himself. Then, after the mandatory two years had passed and after the work was done, he sold the house for top dollar. He never even had to file a tax return if that was his only income. It was all tax-free and it gave him plenty of time to find new deals.

Living in Your Asset

Every homeowner who bought right is sitting on tax-free money right now. Perhaps you are in a market that has gone down, but you know that you bought lower than most of your neighbors. If that's the case, then you know that when the market turns around, you'll be sitting well. Or maybe you are already safe in the knowledge that your house is your biggest asset because it has gone up so much. It isn't an asset unless it puts money in your pocket. But it could be the source of building a tremendous asset base for you. And, you can do it tax-free!

The IRS lets you sell your principal residence in which you have lived two out of the past five years and take out the gain tax-free up to $500,000 if you are married filing jointly or $250,000 if you are single.

Wealth-Building Idea

"I can tell you exactly why I want to hire your firm," Steve began in our initial meeting to review the strategy we had designed for him and his wife.

I sat back to listen. I could tell already that Steve and Corrine were going to be great clients—the type who knew and said exactly what they wanted without wasting their time or mine. I also knew this trait would make them millionaires. I wondered why they weren't already.

"I am a very successful doctor," Steve continued. "You saw our tax returns—I cleared over $500,000 last year, but the minute the insurance or managed care companies change their rules, our income will suffer. This may sound extravagant, but I just don't see how we can live on less than $30,000 per month. I know a lot of people live on a whole lot less—but I just don't want to ever have my family have to settle for less. So I'm here to look at ways I can build something that will survive the lean times."

"Steve knows real estate," Corrine said. "We have a friend named Jack who is a terrific real estate broker. Our friend makes other people a lot of money and that's what I'd like to have him do for us. In fact, I know he has an undervalued apartment complex right now that needs $250,000 in investment for the down payment. I know Jack. He won't let that deal go by and so he'll do what he's always done—get on the phone and make one of his clients a lot of money."

Steve nodded his head. "This guy is really good and I trust him. I want him to make us some money this time!"

"So, this is what I'd like to do," Corrine said clearly. "We have a lot of built-up appreciation in our house and there are other deals out there. I'd like to sell our house. We paid $400,000 two years ago and have put about $50,000 into upgrading it. I think we could easily sell it for $1 million. Meanwhile, Jack could find us another undervalued house and we could do it again."

"However," Steve protested, "I don't want to buy a house for over $1 million. But if we don't, then we'd lose everything to taxes. That's why we're here—to find out if there are some tax loopholes so we don't have to keep buying bigger and bigger houses."

"Wait, I can help you there," I said. "Steve, I think you are referring to some old tax law. You and Corrine can now take $500,000 out tax-free from your house. And you don't even have to invest it in anything. You're absolutely right—the old law said that you had to buy a house of equal or greater value. But that's all been changed."

I turned to Corrine. "Corrine, I want to go through the numbers briefly. You paid $400,000 for the house—right?"

She nodded.

"Okay, we'll need to look at the original escrow statement from when you bought the house. I'm sure there are some additional costs that we can add to that basis. That would include the closing costs, for example." I paused while Corrine made a note of the request. "Oh, Corrine, please look up the actual costs of items that went into the re-modeling. We can add those to the basis as well. What do you think the house will sell for?"

Steve paused to think, then said, "I would say $1 million is probably a fair number. I think I see where you are going. You're trying to make sure we stay under the $500,000 gain. If we actually sold for $1 million and the cost plus improvements was $450,000, we'd have a taxable gain of $50,000. No big deal, really."

"Steve, you're right on track. But I'm thinking that probably with the closing costs when you bought the house increasing the basis *plus* the cost to sell that extra gain will be wiped out.

"We have one more item to consider in our planning. We need to determine how much another house would cost, what cash you can plan on receiving from the house, and what cash requirements you would have. Once you have that information, let's sit down and put a pencil on this undervalued apartment building," I finished.

"Let's talk on Friday," Corrine said. "I can get all that information together very quickly."

I smiled. They *were* fun clients.

Previous Law

I am still amazed at how many taxpayers aren't aware of the greatest tax gift Congress has ever given us. That tax gift is the ability to build up equity in your personal residence and then sell it without paying taxes. The previous law, which unfortunately is still believed to be current, stated that you had to reinvest in a more expensive house unless you had reached a certain age. As I speak at seminars across the country, I find that at least ten people will question me on this tax law change.

The new (five years old!) tax law is that if you live in your house for two of the previous five years, you can take advantage of the tax-free income. You don't have to buy another house. You don't have to be a certain age. It is available to every homeowner in the country.

Calculating the Two-Year Holding Period

The rule is that two of the previous five years must have been used as the principal residence. The five-year period runs backward from the date of the sale of the property. During that five-year period, a total of two years (730 days) must have been used for personal use. Short temporary absences for vacations or seasonal absences are counted as periods of use, even if the individual rents the property out during these periods of absence. Note that any absence over one year is not considered a temporary absence.

For a married couple, the ownership test is met if either spouse meets the test's criteria. However, if one of the spouses has taken advantage of this on another property within the previous two years, the couple must wait two years to take advantage of this exemption on the current property. Otherwise, the gain exclusion is limited to $250,000 (the amount of exclusion for a single taxpayer).

HOW DOES AN EMPLOYEE TAKE ADVANTAGE OF LOOPHOLES?

A frequently asked question during interviews is "How does an employee take advantage of loopholes?" The answer is to take advantage of this tax-free gift from Congress! If you have a knack for decorating, renovating, or simply know how to find a good deal, then consider taking advantage of this loophole. The only drawback is that you have to move every two years. But that move could simply be down the road to the next deal. Meanwhile, consider what your life could be like with gaining tax-free income.

WHAT IF I DON'T LIVE IN THE HOME FOR THE MANDATORY TWO YEARS?

The IRS provides for hardship relief in certain cases where a taxpayer has to sell their home prior to the two-year time frame. The IRS tells us (at IRC Section 121) that:

> if the sale or exchange of the residence is due to a change in the taxpayer's place of employment, health, or, to the extent provided in regulations, unforeseen circumstances, a taxpayer who does not otherwise qualify for the exclusion is entitled to a reduced exclusion amount.

The IRS defines "unforeseen circumstances" as involuntary conversion of the home, natural or manmade disasters or acts of war, death, cessation of employment, change in employment or self-employment, divorce or legal separation, or multiple births resulting from the same pregnancy.

The "reduced exclusion amount" means that you can then exempt an amount equal to either the pro-rata portion of time lived in the house times the total possible gain exclusion, but no more than the total gain. In other words, let's say that John and Corrine had only lived in their home for one year and had reason under this clause to qualify for the special circumstances. The fraction allowable would be 50 percent (1 year divided by 2 years). They could then take an exemption for half of the possible gain (50 percent × $500,000 = $250,000). If they had a gain of $100,000, they could exclude all of it. If they had gain of $300,000, they could only exclude $250,000.

Business Use of Your Home

There is one possible problem that can occur when you take advantage of the home office deduction for your business. This deduction is a great way to write off expenses that you normally wouldn't get—such as home insurance, utilities, private mortgage insurance, homeowner's dues, and the like—as you apply the business percentage of your total square footage.

There is one more reason to consider using your home office as a deduction. The miles you put on your vehicle traveling from your home to your place of business is considered a commute. Once there, your additional travel for business purposes is considered business. However, having your business in your home means that your "non-deductible commuter miles" are now just a short stroll down the hall. Everything from that office to other places of business is then completely deductible.

Taking a home office deduction is a great tax reduction strategy. And, contrary to public opinion (or misinformation), it will not put the $500,000 (for married filing jointly) capital gain exclusion in jeopardy.

The IRS tells us that if the home office is part of the same "dwelling unit" as the home, then there is no need to attribute part of the gain to the sale of the principal residence. If you have taken a depreciation deduction for that part of the home, then you will need to recapture the depreciation upon sale. But that's it! You do not need to pay capital gains tax on the sale.

If the home office is in a separate dwelling unit (such as a separate building that is not connected or a "basement apartment" that could be rented out) then you will need to apportion the gain upon sale. You will then need to pay tax on that portion of the gain.

Loss on Your Principal Residence

What if the unthinkable happens and your home goes down in value? The best advice is probably to wait it out and sell when the real estate market takes an upswing. There are many areas in our country, such as parts of California and Arizona, where the real estate market can have wild fluctuations. If you find yourself in a downswing, wait for the upswing.

There could be circumstances when you don't expect the market to turn back for your house or a situation where you just have to sell. If that's the case, and there is absolutely no other alternative, you may get stuck with a loss that you can't take on your tax return.

You are not allowed to take a loss on your principal residence, but you can take a loss on a business or investment property.

One strategy could be to convert your depreciated home into a rental property, making sure it legitimately can be characterized as such, and then sell it for the lesser value. The loss would be calculated as the sales price less the cost of the sale minus the basis. The basis would be what you had invested in the house during the time you owned it personally. In this way, you could take a deduction for the loss.

What if Gain Exceeds Tax-Free Amount?

Here's the best problem of all! What if your gain exceeds the exclusion ($250,000 for single, $500,000 for married filing joint) amount? Beside the obvious answer of "pay the tax and throw a really big party," you could also consider converting your home into a rental property. If the property legitimately is converted (with renters and proven history), then you could IRC Section 1031 (like-kind or Starker exchange) the property into another property. See Chapter 11, "Loophole #4: Sell Now, Tax Later."

Strategy for Highly Appreciated Rental Property

Finally, you can use this gain exclusion as a strategy for highly appreciated rental property that you want to sell. Normally, you would have to either pay tax on capital gains or roll the gain into another property through a like-kind exchange. Instead, though, you could move into the property for two years and then take the gain out tax-free up to the limits. Remember, you will have to pay tax on the recaptured depreciation. Note that if it is a multi-unit complex, this strategy doesn't work, as only the part that is your principal residence will count.

Chapter 9

Loophole #2: Accelerating Depreciation

Phantom Expense

There are three types of income—earned, portfolio, and passive. Earned income is the highest taxed income of these three, potentially taxed at over 53 percent for federal tax alone. Portfolio income (your money works for you) is much better than earned income, at the second highest taxed. The best type of income, from a tax and lifestyle perspective, is passive income. With passive income from real estate, you can receive cash flow (money you put in your pocket each month) and pay no tax. That is due to the phantom expense of depreciation.

The government allows you to take a deduction each year for depreciation, the amount they tell you that your property has gone down in value. The theory of depreciation is that your real or personal property gradually degrades in time. In the case of personal property, such as vehicles, this theory is true. Anyone who has ever purchased a car and immediately seen the value decrease can attest to the validity of depreciation for personal property. But real property is another story. Does it really go down in value? In some areas, yes, but generally, over time real property appreciates. It goes up in value.

This is an example of a loophole that Congress has provided for real estate investors. Even though we know property, if bought right and maintained to its fullest potential, will go dramatically up in value, Congress lets you take a deduction for a reduction in value. The IRS provides tables to calculate how much the depreciation will be for your property.

Classes of Property

First, you will need to classify the class of the property involved with your investment. This is a critical step that, unfortunately, most investors and their accountants do only partially. Here are the steps:

1. Break out the value of the land, separate from the structure. *Tip:* Many times the value of a bare lot in the area plus the cost of the construction does not equal the total purchase price. One tip the professionals use is to compare the assessor's statement of value for the land and building with the purchase price. Use the ratio that the assessor uses for land to building against the total price for your property to determine the ratio between land and building. Land is not depreciable.

2. Break out the value of personal property items within your building. A checklist for these items follows at the end of this chapter. The best way to do this is to have an appraiser help you with the value of these items. If you can't find an appraiser in your area, use the fair market value (FMV) of the personal property items and then compare that value with the total cost of the building. Generally, it's hard to substantiate more than 30 percent to 40 percent of total building value in personal property items. Personal property items are depreciated over a shorter life—typically ranging from seven to fifteen years.

3. The value of the structure is the total price less land less personal property. This is then depreciated as real property. Currently, real property used in residential rental properties is depreciated over twenty-seven and a half years, and real property used in commercial properties is depreciated over thirty-nine years. If property was placed in service prior to May 13, 1993, there will be different depreciation lives.

4. The depreciation for the real and personal property is then subtracted from your operating income for the property. (Operating income means that you have deducted the costs of the property—such as mortgage interest,

property tax, insurance, homeowner's dues, utilities, repairs, as well as your business expenses.)

5. In some states, such as California, you are also required to keep depreciation schedules using the state's assignment of life. This is where you really need to have a good tax software program. Otherwise, you are going to compile a lot of spreadsheets.

How to Catch Up Past Accelerated Depreciation

The step that many taxpayers miss is number two above. They forget to separate the value of the personal property for depreciation purposes. It is estimated, based on the review of past records of new clients of DKA, that over 90 percent of those clients filing the relevant returns make this very common mistake. This costs each taxpayer thousands of dollars. If you have made this mistake in the past, don't despair. You can recover the past depreciation with your next tax return by filing Form 3115 and attaching a statement.

What Happens When You Sell

When you sell your property, you will be required to recapture the depreciation at ordinary income tax rates or capital gains, in some cases. You then pay the capital gains rate on the difference between the basis and the sales price (less costs). Or you can delay the tax through a Section 1031 like-kind exchange.

Common Mistake

Another mistake is much more potentially damaging. Some taxpayers have made the mistake of not deducting depreciation on their investment property. This was discussed previously, but it is a serious error and bears discussing again. If you've made this mistake, correct it immediately by filing to take the past depreciation with your current tax return. If you don't take the depreciation when you should, the IRS will assume that you took it anyway. You'll have to pay tax on the recaptured depreciation even if there's nothing to recapture!

Property Allocation Worksheet

Following is the property allocation worksheet that we use with our clients at DKA. Complete this for each property that you own and give it to your own tax preparer at year end so they can properly allocate the values for the depreciation on your rental properties.

Diane Kennedy's Real Estate Allocation Worksheet

Building: _____

	Allocated Cost	1245—7-year	1250—15-year	1250—39/27.5-Year	Land
Land Costs	_____			_____	____
Paving and Surfacing	_____		_____		
Curbs and Sidewalks	_____		_____		
Site Concrete Work	_____		_____		
Site Piping Service	_____		_____		
Site Improvements and Utilities	_____		_____		
Site Fire Loop Piping System	_____		_____		
Landscaping	_____		_____		
Site Lighting	_____		_____		
Equipment Foundations and Pits	_____	_____	_____		
Building Construction	_____			_____	
Air Walls/Folding Partitions	_____	_____			
Carpet Work	_____	_____			
Protective Specialties	_____	_____			
Loading Dock Equipment	_____	_____			
Cabinetry, Counters, and Millwork	_____	_____			
Process Piping System	_____	_____			
Computer Fire Protection	_____	_____			
Process Ventilation System	_____	_____			
Process Power System	_____	_____			
Emergency Battery Lights	_____	_____			
Public Address/Sound System	_____	_____			
Telephone Equipment System	_____	_____			
Office Equipment Power System	_____	_____			
Security Control System	_____	_____			
Kitchen/Break Room Equipment Power System	_____	_____			
Break Room/Vending Power System	_____	_____			
Dishwasher System	_____	_____			
Kitchen Equipment	_____	_____			
Washer/Dryer	_____	_____			
Other Furniture, Fixtures, and Equipment	_____	_____			
Signage	_____	_____			
Bridge Crane Equipment	_____	_____			
Process Fire Protection	_____	_____			
Computer UPS System	_____	_____			

Chapter 10

Loophole #3: Real Estate Professional

Lost Passive Loss

The real estate professional designation solves a problem for many high-income taxpayers—the problem of the lost passive loss. As you learned in Chapter 9, "Loophole #2: Accelerating Depreciation," there are techniques for creating paper losses for real estate that may have nothing to do with whether you make cash flow from the property. This chapter will discuss the loophole of becoming a real estate professional so that you can take full advantage of *all* real estate losses against all other forms of income.

Deducting Real Estate Losses—Tax Client

Frank was a highly paid doctor and his wife, Jill, didn't work outside the home. She was interested in taking over management of their rentals, and if we were able to qualify her as a real estate professional, they knew they would be able to take a full write-off of their passive real estate losses against Frank's high earned income. But Jill wanted to make sure she fully understood why it was important for her to be a real estate professional and then what she needed to do to make it fully legal. "Jill," I said, "first, I want to go over why this is important to your strategy. Then, let's go over the rules on what it takes to be a real estate professional. Is that okay?" She agreed.

I explained: "Since the 1986 Tax Reform Act, the amount of passive losses from real estate is limited to $25,000. However, in the case of high-income taxpayers like you two, you cannot offset the losses at all. But there is a loophole. If you are also a real estate professional, then you can offset unlimited losses. We are going to accelerate depreciation on your properties, so we anticipate a lot of paper losses. Since Frank has a more than full-time career, it would be almost impossible to qualify him as a real estate professional." I paused a minute. It looked like we were all on the same page, so I continued. "Here's the trick for you two. Since you file a tax return together, if we can qualify Jill as a real estate professional, all of the losses will then be offset by the total income on the return. Does that make sense?"

"So," Jill asked, as way of confirmation, "it doesn't matter if Frank is the one who earned the income: Because we are married, we get to take the full deduction?"

I confirmed that Jill and Frank would be able to take the full deduction. This meant that it was important to take the real estate professional designation. Now, it remained to explain to Jill what that meant and make sure she would do the proper activities and record keeping needed.

You must pass two tests to determine if you are a real estate professional. These are two tests that you really want to pass, because you then can pick up flow-through real estate losses that might otherwise be lost due to income or passive activity ceilings.

Hours Requirement

If you are married and file a joint return, then only one spouse needs to pass these two tests. *But,* they must pass the tests alone, based on their own time and activities. This is one test that you can't get help on.

The two tests are:

1. More than half of the time you spent performing personal services in *all* trades or businesses was spent doing "qualified real estate activities."

AND

2. More than 750 hours for the year were spent in "qualified real estate activities."

NUMBER ONE: MORE THAN HALF YOUR TIME

If you have a regular job, as evidenced by a W-2, you will have the burden of proof to show that you worked more in "qualified real estate activities" than you did in your regular job. That means you will have to prove that you worked more than 2,080 hours in the year as a real estate professional, if you had a full-time job. If you didn't have a full-time job, but still have a W-2, you will need to additionally show the number of hours you worked in your part-time job. Remember that if the IRS questions you, they will always assume the worst, and in this case, that means that you worked full-time at the other job. Good records are essential to prove this.

If you have no other outside employment, and no obvious trade or business (such as with a Schedule C), then you only need to pass test number two.

TEST NUMBER TWO: MORE THAN 750 HOURS

First, you must pass test number one, which may have a higher hour requirement. Assuming that you did not have another job that occupied you more than 750 hours in the year, you must prove that you worked 750 hours within the calendar year in "qualified real estate activities."

The question now is: What is a "qualified real estate activity"?

Qualified Real Estate Activity

"Qualified real estate activity" is anything you do in which you "develop, re-develop, construct, reconstruct, acquire, convert, rent, operate, manage, lease or sell" real estate.

Remember, the key is that you perform personal services in these activities, but you don't necessarily have to be the one performing the work. You can be supervising, meeting, planning—all of the activities that go into running a business.

• *Develop:* This would include meeting with engineers, architects, planners, equipment operators, construction personnel, drafters, financial professionals, accounting and legal professionals, and so on, to discuss and implement development of property.

You could also be involved in actually performing some of the development work yourself, if you have such skills, or it could be time you spend hiring professionals, supervising their work, reviewing plans, and/or inspecting the work.

This development could be anything from subdividing property, with no additional amenities added, to actual construction of real property.

• *Redevelop:* This would include meeting with engineers, architects, planners, equipment operators, construction personnel, drafters, financial professionals, accounting and legal professionals, and so on, to discuss and implement demolition of structures and/or redevelopment of the property.

Again, you could be involved in actually performing some of the development work yourself, if you have such skills, or it could be time you spend hiring professionals, supervising their work, reviewing plans, and/or inspecting the work.

• *Construct:* As before, any meetings, planning, hiring, firing, supervision, or inspection of any phase of construction is considered performing this activity.

• *Reconstruct:* Just as with constructing, qualified activities under reconstructing are any that are necessary to this phase of building.

• *Acquire:* Acquiring a property has many phases—meeting with salespeople, looking at a whole range of properties, preparing an offering, responding to counteroffers, arranging financing, meeting with insurance agents, inspections, and actually closing on a property. You don't need to acquire a property to rack up a lot of hours in this area.

• *Convert:* Conversion of property is similar to redevelopment or reconstruction, but might have the additional time element of meeting with planning officials. All of that time counts toward your qualified real estate time.

• *Rent:* The time spent meeting with your property managers to establish rental criteria, as well as acting as renting agent yourself (including the showing, screening, advertising, and so on), will count as qualified real estate time.

• *Operate:* If you spend time as a property manager, or meet with your property manager, then you will spend significant time as the operator of real estate.

• *Manage:* Similar to operation of real estate, if you manage your property, its tenants, prospective buyers, and so forth, then you are involved in qualified real estate activity.

• *Lease:* The time spent meeting with your property managers to establish leasing criteria, as well as acting as renting agent yourself (including the showing, screening, advertising, and so on), will count as qualified real estate time.

- *Sell:* All of the activities involved in selling a property (getting ready for sale, setting up open houses, placing ads, meeting with real estate brokers and prospective buyers, among other activities) count toward qualified real estate time.

Proof of Being a Real Estate Professional

It is important that you keep good track of the time you spend. We recommend that you keep a diary that proves the hours. You can keep track of the activity in your PDA or with a paper system. A sample of the paper diary that we show to clients appears at the end of this chapter.

Real Estate Professions

In some cases, the work you perform already could classify you as a real estate professional. Some possible real estate professional classifications are:

- Real estate appraiser
- Civil or structural engineer
- Real estate agent
- Real estate broker
- Real estate attorney
- Mortgage broker or banker
- Construction trades (landscaper, gardener, general construction, electrician, and the like)
- Architect

Do not count personal services you performed as an employee in real property trades or businesses unless you were a 5 percent owner of your employer. You were a 5 percent owner if you owned (or are considered to have owned) more than 5 percent of your employer's outstanding stock, or capital or profits interest.

Qualified Real Estate Activity Log

Name: _____

Time Period: _____

Other Non–Real Estate Business Activity?   Y / N

If yes, hours spent: _____

Date	Time Spent	Activity (What, Where, Who)
_____	_____	_____
_____	_____	_____
_____	_____	_____
_____	_____	_____
_____	_____	_____
_____	_____	_____
_____	_____	_____
_____	_____	_____
_____	_____	_____
_____	_____	_____
_____	_____	_____

Chapter 11

Loophole #4: Sell Now, Tax Later

Calculating Gain on Sale

You've gotten an offer on your property and you want to sell. Now what? Before you accept the offer, you might want to calculate how much money you will make from the sale.

As discussed previously, the taxable gain on the property is calculated as the difference between the depreciated basis (basis minus total depreciation allowed or allowable). The recaptured depreciation is taxed at ordinary rates, or capital gains rates, and the rest is taxed at the applicable capital gains rate.

Costs of the sale are deducted from the gains. For investment property, this includes everything that costs you money through the close of escrow such as commission, title insurance, transfer tax, and the like. You may also have some accrued mortgage interest and property tax costs. These will be deducted from the final calculation of rental income of the property.

If you have a previously suspended loss (due to unallowed passive loss) on the property, this will also be taken as an expense in the final return.

Warning

A common mistake that sellers make is calculating how much cash they will make on the sale and assuming that the amount received at sale is the taxable gain. If you have refinanced properties (which is used as a wealth-building strategy), you may be in a bad position when you sell. You may even have more tax due (based on the basis when you bought the property) than the amount you receive in cash at the sale because you have taken out cash tax-free during refinancing.

Determining the Basis of the Property

A critical element to determining the amount of gain due is first determining the basis of the property. Basis begins with the purchase price of the property, with other items added or subtracted from the basis. You will need to keep evidence of the basis and its additions and subtractions until the property is sold.

ADDITIONS TO BASIS
The basis is increased by:

- Capital improvements, such as a new roof, new air conditioning, or any major improvements
- Brokers' commissions
- Lawyers' fees (in conjunction with the purchase)
- Costs spent defending or perfecting title
- Zoning costs
- Settlement fees and closing costs
- Installation of utility services
- Title search
- Recording fees
- Survey's transfer taxes
- Owner's title insurance
- Amounts owed by the seller, but paid by the buyer (back taxes or interest)
- Recordation fees

- Assumed mortgage
- (NOTE: Real estate property taxes are a current deduction for the buyer)

REDUCTIONS TO BASIS

The basis is reduced by:

- Depreciation
- Percentage depletion (applicable for mineral property)
- Easements (payment that is received in exchange for granting an easement)
- Canceled debt

Inherited Property

There are additionally special rules related to inherited property. Currently, the beneficiary receives property at a stepped-up basis. In other words, their basis in the property is the fair market value of the property at the time of death. If the property is sold, distributed, or disposed of within six months of death, the value that is used in determining basis is the value of the property at disposition. NOTE: The estate tax rules are dramatically changing. See your tax advisor for current information in this area.

How Do I Avoid Paying Tax on the Gain?

After you've determined how much gain you will have to pay on the sale of your investment property, you might make the decision that you don't want to pay all that tax right now. There are some techniques available to postpone (or avoid) tax, such as: (1) like-kind exchange, (2) charitable remainder trust, (3) installment sale, or (4) incomplete contract for sale.

Like-Kind Exchange—John and Marcia Make Some Money

"I know our plan was to build up passive income," said John in our monthly tax coaching phone call, after making sure he had sent the proposed sales figures and costs for the sale to me, "but I've got an offer on the little four-plex that we bought a year ago. Frankly, the offer is more than the property is worth and I'm concerned with what's going to happen in the area when the new warehouse district goes in. I think I need to take this offer!"

I was really happy with the phone call for a lot of reasons. I wasn't sure how well we would work together in the beginning of our calls. He had a lot of ideas and jumped around in his plans. But he had listened (a great attribute in a client) and now always kept his plan in mind when we talked. I knew he would succeed based on that one change in how he planned his financial future. Plus, he knew that we, as his tax advisors, needed information before we could give advice.

"John, it sounds like you did a good job researching this. Now let's talk about what we can do to minimize the taxes if you do sell. Let's start by talking about a Section 1031 exchange. This is also known as a Starker exchange or like-kind exchange. Are you familiar with this, John?"

"I know just enough to be dangerous. Can you explain it and assume I don't know anything about it?"

"The best way I can describe a 1031 exchange," I explained, "is that it's like when we used to play Monopoly and would trade in the four green houses for one red hotel. That's a 1031—you exchange one or more property for one or more other properties. There are some rules—you need to transfer all of the cash you receive from the sale plus you need to buy a property that costs at least as much as what you sold. Otherwise, you will have some tax due."

1031 EXCHANGE—AN EXAMPLE

A possible scenario could be that you have a rental that you have owned for a number of years. You originally purchased it for $100,000 and you have accumulated depreciation of $40,000. That means your basis in the property is now $60,000 ($100,000–$40,000). Let's say you now get an offer of $200,000 for the house and decide to sell it. After the mortgage on the property of $55,000 and the commission and cost of sale of $15,000, you would net cash of $130,000. However, you would also have tax due on the $125,000 gain from the property. And, $40,000 of that $125,000, representing the depreciation, is possibly taxable at a higher rate.

CASH RECEIVED

Sale Price	$200,000
Cost of Sale	(15,000)
Mortgage	(55,000)
Cash Received	$130,000

GAIN ON PROPERTY

Sale Price	$200,000
Cost of Sale	(15,000)
Basis in Property	(60,000)
Gain	$125,000

You could pay the tax based on the gain on the sale of the property ($125,000), or you could do a like-kind exchange. We'll complete the example with your decision to invest the cash you received into an apartment building. You know you want to buy an apartment building, but you don't know yet which one you want. That's okay. You first let the title company and your agent know that you want to do an exchange. They will help you find an exchange facilitator who will serve to hold the proceeds from the sale of the residential rental property while you look for your replacement property. You have to file a notice within forty-five days that you intend to exchange your property and list possible replacements.

You must close on a replacement within 180 days of the sale of the first property and you must invest all of the cash proceeds and all of the sales proceeds into another property. If you do not, the portion that you keep is called "boot" and will be taxable. You still have the opportunity to roll over the rest of the gain.

Remember, though, that this is a tax-deferred transfer. You have taken the basis of the previous property and transferred it into the new property, so the gain of $125,000 has been rolled into the new property.

You may have taxes due when you sell the second property. In this case, the taxes would be due on both the gain of the second property as well as the gain from the sale of the first property.

There are two possible solutions to avoiding this tax:

1. Roll the sale of the second property into another like-kind exchange; or
2. Sell the property through a CRT (charitable remainder trust).

BEFORE YOU DO A 1031 EXCHANGE

The idea of getting money for a sale and not paying immediate tax is appealing to many people. However, there are some things to consider before you begin a like-kind exchange:

1. Consider the current capital gains rate. If your property would fall under the low 18 percent (or even lower 8 percent) tax rate, it might be advisable to simply pay the tax. That is the lowest rate that we have seen in the U.S. for many years. It might not be that low in the future.

2. Consider the depreciation on the new property. You will roll over your basis into the new property. This means that your depreciation possibilities will be limited by this rolled-over basis. For example, assume that you are exchanging a property currently worth $4 million (with a basis of only $1 million) into a property worth $6 million. You only have a total basis now of $3 million (the rolled-over $1 million plus the difference between the value of $4 million and $6 million). As your investments mature (and the depreciation adds up), your basis will continue to diminish. At some point, like-kind exchanges might not make tax sense since you will lose the ability to deduct the phantom depreciation loss.

3. Consider the requirements of the like-kind exchange. There are very specific rules for a proper 1031 exchange. This is a very easy test to fail. These restrictions may make it difficult for you to enact the like-kind exchange.

4. Consider the cost of the like-kind exchange. You will want to have a qualified intermediary handle the exchange, and there is a cost associated with doing that. If you don't have much gain that you are deferring, the cost may not justify going through the steps for a small tax savings now.

5. Finally, make sure you have a good team to help you with this tricky transaction. It's an easy transaction to do wrong!

SETTING UP FOR A 1031 EXCHANGE—NEW RULES

Sometimes partners come together to buy a single property. Many times they hold their joint interests in some form of partnership, such as a limited partnership (LP) or a limited liability company (LLC). In the past, if you had an LP or LLC with multiple owners and the partners wanted to exchange into another property, then the LP or LLC itself would exchange for a property. In other words, the partners stayed the same and the only thing that changed was the property. You couldn't sever one partner's interest from the others and partially exchange only part of the property. There was a great deal of confusion regarding joint ownership of property and how to properly exchange property when there were multiple owners with multiple plans.

The new rules just issued by the IRS state that multiple owners in a property must hold title "in common" with a maximum of thirty-five owners with no entity treatment (cannot be held in a partnership or other business entity) on the property. For asset protection, each owner should have a single-member LLC hold their particular ownership. In this way, one owner can then exchange his or her piece only into a new property. The ownership can be severed for 1031 purposes.

GETTING MONEY OUT OF A 1031

As stated earlier, you are required to roll over all of the cash you might receive from a 1031, as well as the basis. In other words, if you have a property with a large amount of equity, you are required to roll that equity into the next property. It might seem like a good idea, then, to take out a loan on the property just before you transfer. Unfortunately, the rules of the 1031 exchange say you can't do that. But what you can do is take out a loan on the property that you received. In other words, do the 1031 exchange, get the new property, and then refinance. This is one loophole that will allow you to get the cash from the 1031 exchange.

BACK TO JOHN

"What happens when I want to sell the second property?" John asked. "Is the plan to just keep rolling these forever?"

"Well, one possible problem that will occur with the 1031 exchanges," I answered, "is that as you keep rolling into new properties, your basis doesn't increase unless you pay more for the next property. In other words, if you sell for $200,000 and roll into the next property for $300,000, you will have picked up $100,000 in basis. Otherwise, your basis in the next property would be the same as the property that you sold. At some point, the property would be fully depreciated. One of the benefits of real estate is being able to take advantage of the phantom expense—depreciation—so another strategy may be to take advantage of a charitable remainder trust, a CRT."

"Is that something I could do now?" John asked.

"Maybe . . . let's go through what is involved with doing a CRT," I responded. I paused a second, reflecting, before continuing. John had turned into a great client. His questions made sense, he was thoughtful . . . and to think I almost fired him in the beginning! He may very well be changing my mind about Harvard MBAs.

Charitable Remainder Trust (CRT)

A charitable remainder trust (CRT) is an irrevocable trust that provides for and maintains two sets of beneficiaries. Note that this is an *irrevocable* trust, in other words, you can't change your mind once the CRT is put in place. You can change the charitable beneficiary and under certain circumstances can serve as the trustee to maintain full investment control of the asset.

The two beneficiaries are (1) income beneficiaries and (2) charitable beneficiaries. The income beneficiaries will receive a specified amount of income during your lifetime and the charity will receive the principal (in the language of law—the corpus) at your death.

HOW A CRT WORKS

The CRT strategy is a good one for someone who has a highly appreciated piece of property, a charitable mind-set and is open to legal, creative tax solutions.

The property is donated to the CRT. The taxpayer then receives an income tax deduction based on the calculated present value of the remainder interest that the charity will receive.

The CRT can then sell the asset, and because of its charitable intent, will not pay tax on the sale. That means every dollar from the sale is now available to invest for the benefit of the income beneficiaries.

The amount that the income beneficiary will receive depends on the payout percentage and the amount of income the assets generate within the CRT. The IRS states that a minimum amount must be distributed (currently 5 percent of the fair market value of the assets). Many CRTs are set up to pay income of 10 percent to the beneficiaries.

This asset is also now considered "outside of your estate." This means that it would not be included for estate tax.

WARNING: You have just moved a piece of your estate out of your ownership. Your heirs will not receive the benefit of the asset. Many taxpayers supplement this with life insurance to make up the difference.

OTHER CRT STRATEGIES

It is possible to set up the CRT so that your heirs will receive the remainder upon your death and the charity receives the income during your lifetime. You will still receive the current income tax deduction (charitable donation) and reduction of capital gains taxes. This plan is known as a charitable lead trust (CLT).

Installment Sale

Another tax deferment strategy is with the installment sale. Under the installment method, gain from an installment sale is prorated and recognized over the years in which payments are received. The installment sale can only be used for nondealers.

Incomplete Contract for Sale

Under present law, a dealer cannot use the installment sales reporting method for reporting sales and paying tax. This means that the dealer will pay the tax without having the money for any completed sale. One solution for the dealer is to use the incomplete contract for sale.

In order to understand how this works, first let's examine what makes up a completed contract. The IRS has stated in a Private Letter Ruling that the determining factors for a completed sale are:

> In general, where a sales contract provides for installment payments, with the legal title remaining in the vendor until the payment of the last installment, the following factors are relevant in determining when the sale is complete:
>
> (1) Whether the amount of and right to the purchase price is fixed and unqualified.
> (2) Whether the obligation to convey title on final payment of the purchase price is absolute.
> (3) Whether the vendee has taken possession or has the legal right to possession.
> (4) Whether the vendee has otherwise assumed the benefits and burdens of ownership.

It is clear that the presence of all of these factors would compel the conclusion that a sale has occurred; moreover, since a single factor is not controlling, the absence of any of them would not compel the conclusion that a sale had not occurred.

FIXED AND UNQUALIFIED AMOUNT OF AND RIGHT TO THE PURCHASE PRICE

This is a tough requirement to overcome. Face it, if you have a contract, you're going to want it to spell out how much you will receive and when you will receive it. Remember though that the court is going to look at all the factors. So you will want to flunk some of the other tests if you want to prove an incomplete contract.

OBLIGATION TO CONVEY TITLE

Read the requirement by the IRS very carefully. The key word is "absolute." If your contract has a "no recourse" clause, it looks like the IRS won't consider this a completed contract. Specifically, one Tax Court case has told us that "the taxpayers never had an unqualified right to recover the consideration for their old residence . . . until they were paid in full." The contract specifically stated that there was "no recourse." In this case the Tax Court said that there was not a completed contract. But it isn't quite that easy. The appeals court overturned the decision, because "the Tax Court . . . was wrong as a matter of law in relying upon a single item as the determining factor concerning the date of sale." They further said, "No recourse paragraph should be looked on as only one of the conditions of the total transaction."

This means this is a factor, but only one of the factors.

WHETHER VENDEE HAS RIGHT TO POSSESSION

Chances are your buyer has this right, so there is no hope for relief here. Please note that the term *vendee* and *buyer* are interchangeable.

WHETHER BUYER HAS BENEFITS AND BURDENS OF OWNERSHIP

We're down to the fourth possible out of the completed contract. With the no recourse language, we need one other proof to get out of the completed contract for dealers. Here are the questions that determine the benefits/burdens of ownership:

Does the buyer:

- Have the right to possess the property?
- Have responsibility for insurance?
- Have the right to rent the property?
- Have the duty to maintain the property?
- Bear the risk of loss?

- Have the obligation to pay taxes, assessments, and charges against the property?
- Have the right to improve the property without the owner's consent?
- Have the right to obtain legal title?

If the answer to all or most of the above is no, then you have an incomplete contract. This means that a dealer does not have to recognize gain until all money is received, similar to the installment sales reporting method.

Tax-Deferral or Tax-Free?

The strategies above are for tax-deferral. There is a day of reckoning for the tax for each of the plans, with the exception of the CRT or CLT. Another way to build your real estate wealth is through taking money out of your property without paying tax. We'll talk about that more in the next chapter.

Chapter 12

Loophole #5: Getting Money Out of Your Property

Wealth-Building Program

If your goal with real estate investing includes wealth building, then one powerful strategy is to use the full value of the property. Property bought well appreciates. That appreciation can be used to build additional wealth as demonstrated below. WARNING: The property investment must be fundamentally sound to make this work. I have heard people swear to hang on to any investment they have made, even when it makes no sense otherwise as an investment. It is possible to have a property with positive cash flow (or at least neutral cash flow) and still have appreciation. Don't sacrifice cash flow for appreciation. That's a risky route to take.

As shown previously in Chapter 1, "Why Invest in Real Estate?," debt, also known as leverage, can be powerful when you are building wealth. If you have $20,000 to invest in a $200,000 property that appreciates at 5 percent, you can either have a little over $400,000 or over $6 million! The biggest results come when you use your banker's money to grow your wealth.

Should You Pay Your Property Off?

With the amazing returns shown above (turning $20,000 into over $6 million), people still think the safe route is to pay off property debt as soon as possible. Why is that so touted? I believe the secret comes from understanding the cash flow patterns of the poor, middle class, and wealthy as discussed in *Rich Dad Poor Dad,* by Robert Kiyosaki and Sharon Lechter, CPA.

If you look carefully at these cash flow patterns, you see that the poor pattern is to have income and expenses—no assets and no debt. The risky middle-class pattern is to have no assets, but plenty of liabilities. Many people have moved solidly into the middle-class pattern and want out. They are looking at buying assets simply so they can move back to where they are comfortable—the poor pattern of no debt. It is not a question of wanting to be (or act) poor; it is more an issue of not feeling comfortable managing debt. The difference with real estate investing is knowing the difference between good debt and bad debt. Real estate debt is good debt. With leverage, you use other people's money to build assets.

If you're uncomfortable managing good debt, then find a way to make that comfortable for you. Managed debt is the way to wealth.

Objection: Real Estate Isn't Liquid

One of the biggest objections stock market investors will use for real estate investing is that it isn't liquid. After all, if you have a stock and want to sell it, you can generally sell that stock in a matter of moments. Real estate may take months to sell.

The answer is to not sell the property! Instead get your liquidity through cash flow and loans. Real estate is the one asset where you can have your cake and eat it, too. You get the cash, and the real estate still works for you.

Chapter 13

Loophole #6:
Real Estate Investing
with Your Pension Plan

Pension Plans for the Future

What is your plan for the future? Is your pension plan going to be enough? The Department of Labor estimates that 96 percent of Americans today will be dependent on someone else when they retire, or severely cut down on their lifestyle. At the same time, most Americans know that Social Security funds, if they are there at all, won't be enough. Yet at the same time, the Department of Labor also estimates that Americans only spend an average of ten hours total preparing for their retirement. If you're willing to invest a little time investing in your retirement, you can escape that 96 percent mediocrity. One way to do that is through the self-directed pension plan.

Types of Pension Plans

You might have heard that you cannot invest in real estate in your IRA accounts because your advisors are confusing the rules of non-ERISA pension plans with those of ERISA (Employee Retirement Income Security Act of 1974). Under ERISA, employer-sponsored qualified plans have limitations on investments such as investment in limited partnerships (no more than 25 percent of a limited partnership can be funded by retirement funds), real estate investing (no), and trust deeds (another no). If you are invested in such a plan, such as a 401(k), you have little or no say as to how the money is to be invested. Sure, you may have a few options of mutual funds or company stock, but other than that, you have little control.

Self-directed pension plans, which include IRAs, Keoghs, SEPs, and Roth IRAs, are not subject to these limitations. Without those limitations, you have control and huge potential. If you currently have one of these types of plans, you can ask your administrator (typically your stock broker) to switch you to a self-directed plan. If they won't do that—move your money!

The money that you earn from your self-directed plan might be either deferred (in the case of IRAs, Keoghs, and SEPs) or tax-free as in the case of the Roth IRA.

What Can You Invest In?

It's probably easiest to list what is prohibited. The list is short:

- Insurance
- Collectibles, such as paintings, Oriental rugs, and the like

What does that leave? A lot! You can invest in real estate (whether subdivided projects, improved projects, or bare land), trust deeds, notes, real estate investment trusts, limited partnerships, bonds, mutual funds, and annuities.

If you are looking for investment capital for your real estate projects, it might be as simple as looking toward your self-directed pension funds.

Types of Property Your IRA Can Own

Your self-directed plan can invest in single-family and multi-unit homes, apartment buildings, co-ops, condominiums, commercial property, improved or unimproved land.

Fractional interests in the property may be purchased or sold but these interests must not be bought from the beneficial owner of the plan or members of their family or business. Siblings are allowed, however.

There are a few more restrictions to the plan:

1. You may not personally own property that you intend to purchase with plan funds.

2. You must ensure that your intended purchase is not a prohibited transaction.

3. The property must be purchased for investment purposes only.

4. Neither you, your spouse, nor family members (except for siblings) may have owned the property prior to its purchase.

5. Neither you nor your family members (other than siblings) may live in or lease the property while it's in the plan.

6. Your business may not lease or be located in or on any part of the property while it's in your plan.

Financing Concerns

Your pension plan can have a loan on the property; however, the pension fund must be the signer on the loan and all payments must come from the pension. In reality, this may be a hard loan to come by. Many people use their pension fund instead to purchase property free and clear or to buy options. Following are some strategies you can use to invest your self-directed pension funds in real estate.

Real Estate Strategies

• *Real estate options*: Your pension fund can buy an option on a property from an unrelated party (remember siblings are exempted). The story of Tom and John on page 92 is an example of how an option could work:

• *Retirement property*: Your pension plan could buy the retirement property you've always dreamed of. When you retire, the plan will distribute it to you. The pension plan bought your dream home! Sell your principal residence (tax-free of course) and the proceeds are yours for your retirement.

• *Pooling pensions to buy properties*: Loans are difficult for pension plans, which means that the more expensive properties may be out of reach. But you can pool pension plans with others to buy investments.

• *Limited partnership*: Your pension plan can be a limited partner. There is a potential, however, to generate what's termed unrelated business income that may subject your pension plan to some taxes. The unrelated business income within a real estate partnership would occur, for example, when the partnership secured a loan. Consult with a tax expert to verify how much tax could be incurred for your investment. The deal still may be worth it, particularly in a regular pension (as opposed to a Roth), as the tax would be due eventually anyway.

Tom has found a great deal! It's a real fixer-upper and he could do the work, but he has a problem. He can afford the down payment and will qualify for the loan, but doesn't have the money to do the fix-up and to hold the property while it's under construction. The house will cost $100,000 and will easily be worth $200,000 once the work is done. Tom estimates the materials will cost about $20,000.

His friend John has a suggestion. John has some money in his pension fund that has been steadily losing value. He's ready to invest it in a better deal and this sounds like it.

Tom agrees to buy the home and do the work. He would like to get $20,000 for his work and then split the profit of $60,000 ($200,000 −100,000 − 20,000 − 20,000 = $60,000).

John agrees with the terms and directs his IRA to buy an option for $20,000 to buy the home for $150,000.

When the property sells (assuming the $200,000 sales price), the following occurs:

John's IRA does a simultaneous close to buy the house for $150,000 and sell it for $200,000. John's IRA paid $20,000 for the option up front so it will receive a gain of $30,000. His $20,000 turned into $50,000 and he's ready for the next deal.

Tom receives $150,000 (from John's IRA on the simultaneous close). His gain is $50,000—representing $20,000 for his work and $30,000 for his share of the profit. The $20,000 he received for the option was used to complete the repairs and sell the property. Not bad for a four-month effort!

Chapter 14

Loophole #7: Tips for Qualifying for a Loan

A common question we get at my CPA firm, DKA, is how the client can qualify for a loan after we've successfully minimized his tax. You see, what's good for tax strategy planning (less income!) isn't necessarily good for getting loans. Here are some tips for dealing with the situation.

Types of Loans

First of all consider what type of loan you want. If your credit scores are good, you can likely qualify for a "stated income" or "no docs"—no documents—loan. There might be a slightly higher interest rate for this type of loan, but there is also a whole lot less hassle.

You need to prove that you are self-employed (typically a letter from your accountant can establish this), that you have enough money to close the deal, and that your credit scores are good.

Tips for Loan Qualifying for Business Owners and Investors

If the stated income loan is not for you, there are some techniques you can use to maximize the qualifying income for your loan.

TIP #1: ADD BACK DEPRECIATION

Your loan officer (mortgage broker or mortgage banker) should add back depreciation to your income when counting how much you make from your business. One tip you can use in tax preparation is to capitalize all equipment, including items in the "small tools or equipment" category typically expensed. These items can be deducted using the Section 179 deduction, so there is no change in the net effect of your tax return. (This assumes that you have not maximized the Section 179 deduction already.) The depreciation is added back, whereas the "small tools or equipment" items are not. The result is higher income from the lender's perspective.

TIP #2: PAY ALL POSSIBLE PAYMENTS THROUGH YOUR BUSINESS

If you have a vehicle that is used in your business and is financed, make sure your business writes the check to pay for the vehicle. If the loan on the vehicle is in your name, the debt will show up on your personal credit report and be used against your debt ratio. However, if you can prove that the vehicle was paid by your business, the mortgage company will not count this against your debt ratio.

Be prepared to prove who paid for the vehicle by providing one year's worth of canceled checks for the vehicle.

Bad Credit Rating

What if you've had some previous credit glitches? Talk to your lender. Ask him what you can do to clean the credit report up.

Another suggestion is to contact the reporting companies and see what could be done to clean up the rating. It never hurts to ask!

If you can't get around the past credit problems, consider using someone else's credit by assuming loans through a wrap. You pay them; they pay the loan.

Finally, if you find a deal that has a great return, you can always find someone to come in as a money partner. The key is to prove to the money partner that you know what you're doing and to give them fair exchange for the risk and money they are contributing. You will have the hurdle to overcome of answering why someone should give you money when you had money troubles in the past. Be ready for it with a plan that shows you can be trusted with the investment.

Land Trust

One method of using someone else's credit is by establishing a land trust. The land trust can be set up under the original seller's name and then, without filing, the beneficiary can be changed to you. This is one method for assuming a loan without notification to the lending institute and trigger the due-on-sale clause.

Seller Financing

Finally, there is the old tried and true seller financing. See Chapter 8 for the story of one client who landed a cash-flowing office and multi-unit residential property with no money down. The seller financing is out there—you just need to be tenacious to find it!

Part Three

Introduction to Legal Secrets

You have just learned some of the greatest secrets involved with being a savvy real estate investor—opening and maximizing taxation loopholes to your benefit. Now, equally important, especially in today's litigious society, is knowing and using the legal loopholes necessary to protect the property—as well as you and your family—from the many risks of doing business and dealing with the public.

As Robert Kiyosaki's rich dad taught him, owning real estate is an important component of your financial future. And just as important for Robert's rich dad was the method for holding and conserving that real estate. No one should take the time and expense of building a real estate portfolio just to have it taken away for failing to take the right—and relatively simple—legal steps that the rich dads of the world take every day.

So, as soon as you get that first spark to acquire, own, and manage real estate, you need to begin considering how you will protect it. It is important to recognize that protection, the closing of legal loopholes that can lead to personal liability, must be an integral part of any real estate strategy. And note that protection for our purposes here is very broad. We want to protect not only the property you buy but also your personal property, all of your other real estate, and all of your other assets. We want to completely and comprehensively protect you and your family as well as your collective future.

Why must we be so concerned with protection? Because real estate, for all its greatness as an investment, involves risk. And risk, when not properly managed, can lead to claims, demands, litigation, and money judgments. It can lead to personal exposure of your own assets for the faults of others. As such, one must close the legal loopholes to liability.

What Are Some of the Risks Associated with Real Estate?

Many you know. If a tenant falls on your property, you may be held responsible for allowing a dangerous condition to exist that caused or contributed to the injury. In such a case it pays to have adequate insurance coverage, as we'll discuss. As you also know, tenants can sue for imagined grievances as well. You can almost hear the logic. "You are the landlord. You must have lots of money—how else could you afford to own real estate? I think I've been injured. I know—I'll sue!" Protection against these types of out-of-the-blue claims is also important. (Of course, a step toward eliminating the potential for imagined claims can also be accomplished by treating your tenants with a measure of dignity and respect.) But overall, when you are dealing with tenants you are dealing with the public. And dealing with the public means exposing yourself to the diversity of human thought and emotion. While such depth and difference may result in great art and literature on a global scale, on the other end, when it comes to you owning a few rental properties, it means there can be no guarantee of rational human behavior. Which means that protection is essential. In Chapter 17, we'll discuss the risks you have as a landlord.

What Are Some of the Other Risks Associated with Real Estate Ownership?

Contracts. Agreements. Mortgages. Promissory notes. Real estate involves obligations. These commitments may take many forms but all involve a promise to do something: to buy, to pay, to repair, to lease, to perform. And so a risk in real estate is that you fail to perform according to your promise. Will you be personally responsible for not living up to your promise? It depends. In some cases the answer will be yes, which is why we'll discuss this in greater detail throughout this section.

Another risk involves the condition of your property. For example, when holding vacant land, trespassers on your property may sue for hazardous conditions. And when it comes to hazards involving any property, toxic and other environmental problems can be a huge risk. Innocent property owners have been financially and emotionally wiped out by the incredible expense of environmental remediation and cleanup. It is imperative to understand and close off these types of legal loopholes and liability.

For these and other related reasons you must know the legal secrets the rich have used for centuries to protect themselves when owing real estate. You must have adequate insurance coverage, hold your real estate the right way, and use protective agreements when conducting real estate business. Overall, you must be forever alert to take all necessary steps to shield yourself from personal liability in all your dealings.

An important first step is to protect your own primary residence . . .

Chapter 15

Homestead Exemptions

Ogelthorpe

Ogelthorpe was wrongly accused. He had been framed. The tabloids said he'd killed his wife. He was nowhere near the scene of the crime.

But Ogelthorpe was a celebrity, a public figure. So the tabloids could say whatever they wanted about him. Even if it bore an inexact relation to the truth. Live in the spotlight. Die in the spotlight.

Ogelthorpe had been a star athlete and had used that fame to get into the movies. He was a likable lug and got his fair shot at roles where he played the buddy to the main lead. His celebrity led to endorsement deals and a comfortable, if frenetic, lifestyle on Hollywood's A circuit.

And then murder. He swore to everyone he didn't do it. He loved his wife, in spite of her infuriating, fetishistic love of thousands of lit candles that, on numerous occasions, had almost burned the mansion down.

A jury of his peers found him innocent of murder in a criminal trial. The evidence wasn't there—it didn't fit, so they had to acquit. But his wife's family brought a civil action against Ogelthorpe for the loss of their daughter.

The new jury didn't have to worry about whether Ogelthorpe, the well-known celebrity, should go to jail or not. Their issue was just whether the deceased wife's family should get some money. Ogelthorpe bitterly predicted that in today's blame-everyone-else society, the jury would throw cash at the poor, hurt family. If the money is there, you've got to share. True to Ogelthorpe's prediction, millions of dollars were awarded to the family.

But Ogelthorpe knew some good attorneys. He had partied with the best of them in his years in Hollywood. And these guys knew every trick in the book.

Move to Florida, they said. Use Florida's incredible homestead laws to protect your assets from these ridiculous claims.

Ogelthorpe wondered what a homestead was. His big-dog lawyer explained that it was a way to protect the equity in your house. Homesteads were governed by state law and each state had a different limit.

In California, for example, the homestead exemption was $75,000. If your house was worth $500,000 and your mortgage was down to $425,000, you had $75,000 in equity in your home. A creditor could reach that equity. By filing a homestead with your county recorder you could claim that equity interest for yourself and deter a creditor from trying to go after your house.

But Ogelthorpe pointed out that $75,000 wouldn't help much. His house was a full-scale mansion, valued at $5.2 million, and he held it free and clear.

That's why you move to Florida, his lawyer explained. They have an unlimited homestead exemption. As long as your house sits on a lot no larger than one acre, no one can take your home in Florida, no matter how many millions of dollars of equity you have in it.

And so Ogelthorpe exchanged his expensive home in California for an even more expensive home in Florida. He filed a homestead on his new home and was protected to the maximum extent by Florida law. And in Florida he joined a unique collection of stockbrokers, corporate executives, and other unfortunates who had been severely mistreated by the United States system of justice.

Using the Homestead Exemption to Protect Your Primary Residence

As the case points out, homesteads can be an extremely valuable technique for protecting a very important real estate asset—your personal residence—from the claims of others.

Homestead exemptions were started in Texas in the late 1830s, as a way to induce settlers to leave the United States and come to the then Republic of Texas to develop the land. The incentive was powerful for farmers and ranchers who wanted to secure their land from creditors, and homestead laws soon spread to other states as a useful economic development tool. The benefits of homesteads were used to attract European farmers to the United States in the 1870s and 1880s.

Because each state had (and has) different economic development strategies, each state's homestead law is different. Although the size of the property in acres is usually limited, Texas, Florida, Kansas, Iowa, Oklahoma, and South Dakota allow homesteads for an unlimited dollar amount. Pennsylvania, New Jersey, and Delaware offer no homestead exemptions. A chart detailing each state's homestead exemption laws can be found at www.successdna.com.

As a general rule, a person can only have one valid homestead at a time. Also, homesteads usually only apply to real estate owned and occupied as a principal residence. Subject to that constraint, condominiums and co-ops are generally protected and in some states so are mobile homes.

While each state may have variances, generally a homestead does not protect one against debts secured by a mortgage or deed of trust on the property, IRS liens and the payment of taxes, mechanics' liens, child support, and alimony payments. But for other general creditor claims—business and personal loans, credit card debt, accidents—a homestead can preclude the seizure or forced sale of your personal residence.

In Florida the policy protects homeowners to the greatest extent. The Florida Supreme Court has ruled that converting nonexempt property (cash or other property subject to immediate seizure) to an unlimited exempt homestead (a multimillion-dollar home situated on one acre of land or less) is quite all right, even if the purpose is to defraud an existing creditor. Which is why Ogelthorpe was seen running through airports in a rush to Florida.

With your primary residence protected to the greatest extent possible, it is appropriate to shield yourself from personal liability in all of your other real estate dealings. To fully understand why this must be a part of your future, it is useful to look back in time . . .

Chapter 16

Land Ownership and Notice Requirements

To appreciate what you, the landlord, own, it is necessary to understand the nature of landholdings in medieval England. The property laws of the United States, Canada, Australia, New Zealand, and other former British colonies are all based on what evolved from England's feudal heritage. Back in the eleventh and twelfth centuries—and into the recent past—one's social and political status was completely tied to land ownership. Success in business was not even remotely a factor. Unlike today, you could have the most profitable business of that era, be it a wheelworks, an armory, or a distillery, but if you didn't own land you were a second-class citizen.

Conflicting with this very Anglo mind-set was the several-hundred-year annoyance involving the superseding feudal rights of the crown and various overlords to the land. After the Norman conquest of England in 1066, a gift of land was only for the life of the owner. Upon the owner's death, the land technically reverted to the lord or the crown, who could decide to keep the land or demand a fee before the land was transferred to the deceased owner's heir. This didn't set too well with the landowners of the day. They were working to make the land productive, building homes and outbuildings, improvements that raised the crown's taxes on the land. Who, then, should get the property on the owner's death: the son who helped build up the estate or some wheezing, greedy overlord who, except for flogging the help, had never worked a day in his life?

It took some time, but in 1290 legislation was enacted allowing owners to freely sell or transfer their land as they saw fit without the lord's permission or the payment of fees. Interestingly, just as in modern times where Congress has excused itself from contributing into the Social Security system, tenants on the crown's land had to pay for transfers until 1660.

The free transferability of land was a major step in unshackling the restrictive and inefficient chains of feudal obligations. And with this freedom, real estate became even more precious and worthy of protection. Families sought to protect ancestral lands for generations, even centuries. As a result, real estate ownership came to be measured in terms of time, and the theory of estates, unique to Anglo (and later American and Commonwealth) law, came into being. The word "estate," dating from England's feudal past and heritage, is derived from the Latin word for status. As a modern-day landowner this historical evolution affects you to this day.

Four Types of Ownership

Over the centuries, four types of ownership interests, or estates, in real estate evolved. These are:

- Fee estates;
- Life estates;
- Leasehold estates; and
- Estates at will.

Let's quickly review these estates before considering your status as a landlord.

• *Fee Estates*: The greatest ownership interest in real estate is a fee estate. It provides absolute ownership for an indefinite period of time. Subject to any governmental laws restricting land use, a fee owner may do whatever he or she wants with their land. With fee title, also known as fee simple absolute, you can sell, lease, or give the land away. And when you purchase real estate, you want to be sure you are buying a fee estate—so you too can do whatever you want with it, and later freely transfer it.

• *Life Estates*: A life estate is an interest in real estate lasting for the lifetime of the life tenant. An example helps explain this interest:

Bob owns a rental home in a nice part of town. His elderly mother needs a place to live. Bob grants her a life estate in the rental home, allowing her to live there for the rest of her life. Bob continues to own fee title to the house but possession of the house for his mother's life (the life estate) has been "carved out" of the fee. As holder of the life estate, his mother is responsible for taxes and repairs to the property. Upon his mother's death, possession of the house returns to Bob and the life estate is extinguished.

While sometimes used in American real estate transactions (think of bad kids who would evict Grandma from the beach house if not for her life estate), a life estate is more important in England where it offers the status of ownership.

- *Leasehold Estates:* A leasehold is the right granted by a fee owner (a landlord) to a tenant to possess a parcel of real estate. When a landlord and tenant enter into a lease or rental agreement, a leasehold estate in real property is created and conveyed. While the landlord retains fee title, the tenant obtains the right to possess and use the property for the term of the lease. After touching on estates at will, we will review the various types of leasehold estates.

- *Estates at Will:* An estate at will is not much of an estate. It involves a fee owner allowing a tenant to use a property for free. With proper notice, estates at will terminate at the will of the fee owner.

Leasehold Estates

Tenants can hold four types of leasehold interests, which, consistent with the theory of estates, are categorized by their measure of time and term:

1. *Fixed-Term Tenancy* (also known as a Lease): A lease is a tenancy for a fixed term. In England, a lease is also called an estate for years. When the termination date arrives, the lease and the tenant's right of possession automatically come to an end. By exercising a prenegotiated option to extend or by entering into a new lease, the tenancy may continue.

2. *Periodic Tenancy* (also known as a Rental): A rental agreement is also known as a periodic tenancy. This tenancy continues for successive periods, each equal in their time length, be it year to year, month to month, or week to week. The period of time for measurement is based on the interval between rent payments. For example, an annual rent payment evidences a year-to-year tenancy. The tenancy is terminated by notice given in a timely manner. The most common periodic tenancy is month-to-month. In such cases, timely notice to terminate is a thirty-day notice from either the tenant or the landlord.

3. *Tenancy at Sufferance:* A tenancy at sufferance occurs when, upon expiration of the term, a tenant continues to stay in the premises without the landlord's consent. The tenant is commonly known as a holdover tenant. Without a written agreement requiring the tenant to pay holdover rent, the tenant is only liable for the reasonable rental value for each day the tenant holds over.

4. *Tenancy at Will:* A tenancy at will is similar to an estate at will, whereby the tenant takes possession for an undetermined period with the landlord's consent and no payment terms are specified. The landlord must give the tenant notice to terminate the at-will tenancy. Unless there is an agreement otherwise, the tenancy terminates upon the death of the landlord or tenant.

Notice Requirements

As a landlord, what is one of the greatest issues facing your business? Everyone knows this one: Tenants who fail to pay the rent. To protect yourself from those tenants who would misuse the system to take advantage of you and the shelter you offer, it is important to know the rules on terminating tenancies.

Before exploring this area more deeply, let's first discuss lining up a vital member of your team. As Robert Kiyosaki's rich dad taught him, real estate investing is a team sport. And in the realm of landlord-tenant law, you are going to need a good real estate attorney on your bench, ready to come in when needed. It is hoped that you will never need to evict a tenant. But there is peace of mind in knowing that if it ever became an issue, you'll know exactly whom to call.

So, before buying your first rental property, consider locating a real estate attorney in your area who represents landlords in eviction matters. Ask your CPA, friends, and business colleagues whom they would recommend. Check the free professional directory at www.successdna.com. Consider interviewing one or more of these attorneys to see whom you best click with. Explain that you are lining up a team member for future services. Ask what types of fees they charge for evictions. Tell them, if this is the case, that you are considering handling the simple evictions yourself, but need to know someone to call should a matter turn difficult or ugly. Most attorneys will appreciate your advance planning. And the few attorneys who will want $300 just to meet with you will be saying in so many words that they don't want or need your business, which is useful to know up front. With a good attorney on your team and the information obtained in this book, you are on your way toward being protected.

ALL RIGHT, SO HOW DO YOU EVICT A TENANT?

A key element is notice. The notice requirements vary with each type of leasehold. Remember, leaseholds, like estates, are measured by time. So, conceptually, it makes sense that a time period—or notice—would be a crucial factor. A listing of the notice requirements for all fifty states is found at www.successdna.com. It is important to know that notice can vary according to each type of tenancy.

  • *Fixed-Term Tenancy:* When a fixed term tenancy expires, that is it. No notice needs to be given, since by its terms the tenancy has terminated. The landlord can immediately proceed to evict a tenant holding over.

  • *Periodic Tenancy:* As mentioned previously, notice is to be given in accordance with the period between rent payments. A tenant making weekly payments is entitled to seven days' notice. A month-to-month tenant must be given thirty days' notice to terminate the tenancy. If the tenant stays on after the notice period runs, eviction proceedings may begin.

  • *Tenants at Will:* While each state is different, and be sure to check your own state's laws for any variance in all the notices discussed herein, the general rule is that thirty days' notice to vacate must be given to a tenant at will.

  • *Tenants at Sufferance:* The most important thing to know about this tenancy is that it is the catch-all for all of the leaseholds listed above. Once a lease, rental, or at-will tenancy expires, either automatically or by notice, the tenant's holding is over and a tenancy at sufferance is created. The term is a good one, because with the tenant in possession and not paying rent, you are the one suffering. Besides, it's more polite than the common term, which is "squatter."

No one starts out to create a tenancy at sufferance. Instead, these tenancies occur when the other three types of leaseholds come to an end. As such, a holdover tenant is not entitled to any notice. Eviction proceedings can be brought immediately.

Peggy Sue and Myron

Peggy Sue owned a duplex near the airport, which she rented to three tenants. Angel and José lived in one unit and Myron lived in the other.

Myron worked as a baggage claim handler for one of the big airlines and walked to work. He was not happy with his life and complained about everything, real and imagined. This made him an unpleasant person. Sometimes his monthly rent would be late and he would use every expletive available to blame it on everyone but himself. Particularly galling to Peggy Sue was that Myron complained about jet noise over the duplex in the evening. Peggy Sue didn't understand it. Myron was inundated with jet noise all day at work.

The solution to Peggy Sue was simple. If he didn't like jet noise after work, he should buy a car and live away from the airport. She had told this to Myron whenever he complained, which only made his other complaints about the heat and the hot water even more scalding.

Recently Myron had been trying to stir up Angel and José against their landlord. This made Peggy Sue even more angry. She knew she had to do something about Myron, who was now a problem tenant.

Because Myron was a periodic tenant who paid his rent in monthly intervals, Peggy Sue had learned from her real estate attorney that under her state's law she could give him thirty days' notice to terminate the tenancy. If he failed to move out after thirty days he became a holdover tenant and she could begin an unlawful detainer proceeding to evict him.

Peggy Sue didn't want to wait that long. She very much liked Angel and José and couldn't stand the thought of Myron poisoning her relationship with them for the next month or more. Then she noticed that Myron was once again late with the rent. Her attorney had told her of a strategy to shortcut the thirty-day notice requirement.

Peggy Sue had her property manager serve Myron with a three-day notice to pay rent or quit the premises. The notice stated the exact amount of delinquent rent owed, a specific requirement in many states. The notice also stated that if the tenant did not pay in time the landlord was electing to forfeit the tenant's leasehold and retake the premises. This forfeiture clause is a crucial inclusion in the three-day notice.

On the fourth day Myron showed up and tried to tender payment of the delinquent rent. Peggy Sue refused to accept it. Myron became livid and demanded she accept the rent payment. Peggy Sue stuck to her guns. She told Myron that he had missed the three-day deadline and demanded that Myron vacate the premises. He refused to do so, using every expletive in the process.

Peggy Sue had her attorney file an unlawful detainer action to evict Myron. He claimed he had tried to pay the rent and it was refused. But the court noted that (1) Myron's tenancy was terminated once the three-day notice had expired without the payment of rent, and (2) Peggy Sue elected to forfeit Myron's right to possession.

Myron was evicted.

An important point should be gained from this example. In some cases, you may not have to wait thirty or more days to terminate a tenancy. A tenant default which is material, such as the failure to pay rent, allows for the prompt forfeiture of the tenancy. It should be noted that, in most states, a tenant's failure to pay late charges and the like is considered a minor breach, for which a three-day notice cannot be used. However, certain larger breaches, such as conducting a criminal activity on the premises or destruction of the premises, are entirely appropriate for a three-day notice to quit the premises. The landlord cannot wait thirty days in some extreme situations, especially when the breach, such as destruction, cannot be cured by the tenant. A three-day notice to vacate is delivered, thereby terminating the leasehold and restoring possession to the landlord.

Of course, if the tenant ignores the notice you may still have to bring eviction proceedings. Even then, prevailing in such a proceeding is no guarantee that possession will be returned. You may have to call on the sheriff to do that.

It is important to again remind you that each state's laws are different in this area. For example, some states require a five-day instead of a three-day notice. A summary of state notice requirements is found at www.successdna.com. Please consult with an attorney in your locality for specific rules and local practices. It should also be noted that even with the same laws, many states will differ in the outcome. Myron's case is based on the general rules of both California and Nevada law. However, the courts in each state to a certain degree reflect the collective consciousness of the population. As such, a California court hearing Myron's plea that he tried to pay rent and it was refused may side with the tenant and deny a forfeiture of possession, allowing Myron back into the duplex. In Nevada, the court would most likely politely listen to what Myron had to say, strike the gavel down, and send him packing. It is easier to be a landlord in some states than in others.

Chapter 17

Landlord Liability

The need for protection arises from the duties imposed on landlords in managing their properties. Our next case is illustrative.

Ricardo, Jane, and Mike

Ricardo owned a single-family home with a large, grassy yard in an older section of town. He had originally lived in the house as a single man but when he got married and his wife had triplets, he moved to a larger house. Ricardo kept the smaller house as a rental and had recently rented it to Jane, a single woman, who kept a large Doberman pinscher named Brutus on the property.

Brutus was protective of Jane to the point of being aggressive and fierce. Jane put up "Beware of Dog" signs on the fences surrounding the front and back yards, both to deter unwanted intruders as well as to warn the neighbors.

Ricardo was an active landlord. He frequently drove by the property to inspect it and entered the house once a year to check for any damage. He didn't enjoy his inspections because Brutus was such a menacing presence. Still, Jane always paid the rent on time and was a good tenant.

Early one morning, Mike the neighbor was fetching his paper. Out of the blue, Brutus jumped the fence and savagely attacked Mike. The attack continued until Jane woke up and got out of bed to restrain Brutus. Mike's injuries were significant. He was unable to work for several months.

Mike not only sued Jane but Ricardo as well. This was galling to Ricardo, who used to drink beer and watch football with Mike during his bachelor days when they were neighbors. But Ricardo's attorney explained that it is not at all unexpected. Ricardo owned the house in his personal name. There were assets to be reached.

Mike, through his attorney, claimed that Ricardo knew—or, through the exercise of ordinary care, should have known—that a dangerous condition existed on the property. Mike further claimed that Ricardo had a duty to remedy the dangerous condition by having the dog removed from the property.

Ricardo's defense was that he no longer had control of the premises. When he leased it to Jane she became responsible for such matters. The jury sided with Mike. The fact that Ricardo had actual knowledge of Brutus's fierce and aggressive nature due to his visits to the property and observation of the "Beware of Dog" signs was determinative. Ricardo had the ability to remove the dog by serving Jane with a three-day notice to eliminate the dangerous condition or move out, and he had failed to do so. The jury simply applied the law as it exists in most states. If a landlord has knowledge of a dangerous condition on his or her leased premises and has the ability to remove such condition, then the landlord will be liable for resulting injuries to others.

The Duty of Care

The duty of care has evolved over time to accomplish the goals and benefits of public policy. Public policy is that big-picture vision that guides courts and legislatures to achieve a social good, in this case to prevent unnecessary injuries to innocents like Mike, who just wanted to read his morning paper. Through case law and legislation, by establishing the requirement that landlords exercise reasonable care in the management of their property to prevent foreseeable injuries to others, the public policy of attempting to benefit the broadest segment of society is served. As a result, the duty of care a landlord owes applies to all persons, whether they go upon the property as guests or whether they trespass without permission. Of course the duties owed to persons on one's land without permission tested the flexibility of public policy. Early on, several court decisions held that landlords owed a duty to persons injured while illegally on the property intending to commit a felony. The public outcry led to legislation in many states obviating landlord liability to criminals. If a burglar on his way into Jane's house in the middle of the night were mauled by Brutus, too bad. The dog was doing his job and in most states Ricardo would be free from liability.

That exception aside, a landlord who is aware—or should have been aware—of a dangerous condition will be responsible for injuries suffered on his or her property. And a factor the courts will consider in imposing liability is the availability and cost of insurance to cover the risk. So, ironically, failure to have easily obtainable and reasonably priced insurance can cost you even more. As an overall strategy, it is best to understand and live up to the duty of care, have enough insurance to cover those out-of-the-blue claims that no one can foresee, and then further protect yourself with the right entity.

Duty to Inspect

As part of the duty of care to prevent injury to others, a landlord has a duty to inspect the premises for dangerous conditions. When a landlord renews, extends, or initially enters into a lease agreement, a reasonable inspection of the premises is required. Failure to inspect the property at such time can mean that the landlord will be charged with knowledge of the dangerous condition he or she should have discovered in the inspection.

Dallas and Pete

Dallas was the owner of an acre of vacant land at a busy freeway interchange. Pete was a fruit wholesaler who wanted to open a weekend retail produce stand on the property. The two men entered into a lease agreement whereby Pete agreed to pave one quarter of the property and open the business. Dallas had the right to make yearly inspections of the property and had to give Pete approval before any further improvements are made.

The business was hugely successful. Every Saturday and Sunday people would drive for miles to purchase Pete's fresh produce. The open-air market was alive with activity and in the crush of commerce the concrete floor was frequently littered with produce.

Eighteen months into the business, a customer slipped on some lettuce leaves and fell to the floor, suffering injuries. The customer hired a personal injury attorney, who filed a claim against Dallas.

Dallas couldn't believe he had been sued. He was just the landlord—he didn't cause any produce to be littered about the place for people to fall on. He had no notice that the temporary litter was a dangerous condition.

But the jury saw otherwise on this one, which is loosely based upon a recently decided case in California. Dallas was liable for the customer's injuries if the concrete floor's construction is a dangerous condition or becomes a dangerous condition when produce is littered upon it.

The duty to inspect the premises to make sure it is safe from dangerous conditions arises when:

- The lease is renewed, extended, or initially entered into; or
- The periodic right to inspect or approve of construction is granted to the landlord.

The court found that if the landlord had conducted the yearly inspections as granted in the lease he would have noticed the dangerous condition. Never mind that an inspection during the week when the stand was closed would not have revealed such a problem. A landlord owes a duty to the public to exercise reasonable care in inspecting the property, which meant that a weekend inspection was warranted.

Duty to Disclose a Dangerous Condition

A landlord's duties may extend to an affirmative requirement to warn tenants of existing problems. While perhaps not the law in every state, the following scenario is based on an actual California court case. As has happened over the last fifty years, certain vanguard California decisions, often seen as outrageous in their day, tend to become adopted into the mainstream over time. So, knowing that other states may follow, it is useful to see where the California courts are headed with regard to landlord duties.

Jamal and David

Jamal owned an apartment complex in a decent part of town where recent assaults on local tenants had shocked the neighborhood. Two of the tenants lived in Jamal's complex. Jamal was concerned and met with the police, who gave him a composite drawing of the criminal and a description of his modus operandi. Based on what the police said and the information they had, Jamal felt confident that the perpetrator would soon be apprehended. Still, Jamal thought about having a security service patrol the property until the risk was over.

Later that day, David came to the apartment complex to look at a vacant apartment. Jamal didn't disclose the recent criminal activity and told David that the complex was safe and patrolled by security. David was satisfied with the apartment and entered into a lease with Jamal.

A week after he moved in, David was assaulted by the same perpetrator, this time inside his apartment. David sued Jamal for his injuries claiming that Jamal failed to disclose the recent criminal activity and misrepresented the safety of the complex. Jamal asserted that he was not responsible. The attack didn't occur in a common area, but rather in the tenant's own apartment.

The court ruled in David's favor. With knowledge of criminal activity in the area, the landlord owed a duty to the tenant to either provide adequate security in the common areas or warn of the previous assaults. The court held that Jamal's failure to do one of the two created a risk that David might be injured. David was awarded damages.

It is interesting to note that California's courts have also found home-owners' associations liable for injuries caused by an undisclosed dangerous condition.

Implied Warranty of Habitability

Along with the duty to act reasonably in inspecting and maintaining a property, a landlord has a duty to lease property that is in a condition fit for human occupancy. While this may sound like a given, it took quite a while for the courts to arrive at such a requirement.

Remember our discussion of British feudal heritage? Well, in centuries past some of those landowner types, having estates and status and all, felt that they could offer whatever squalid, wretched corner they pleased to the unlanded citizenry. They should feel lucky to even have a roof over their heads, was the attitude of that era's landlords. Never mind that the roof leaked buckets, year in and year out.

This mind-set prevailed in England, America, and other Commonwealth countries for centuries and was accepted by the courts. Landlords could rent whatever pigsty they wanted. If a tenant didn't like it, they could move on to the next property. The courts routinely supported the landlord's position that if the lease contract did not call for habitable conditions the landlord was not contractually obligated to provide such.

Of course, a problem arose in that with no obligation to rent out property that was fit for human occupancy, not many landlords provided a habitable property. Sure, the tenant could go down the street to the next property, but chances were that it was more foul than the previous place. And with all these unfit hovels with improper heating, sewage, and sanitation spread around town, you had disease incubators for cholera, typhoid, plague, hepatitis, and the like. The landlords collectively created a public health nightmare. These were not the good old days.

When presented with this alarming evidence many landlords of the day were uncaring. Their attitude was still that if the tenant didn't like the property they could go on to the next one. If there was no clean, habitable property to be found, that tenant could just as well move back to their farm or wherever else they came from.

Things have finally changed in recent decades, as the judicial system became more open. Instead of judges who grew up on estates in comfortable surroundings, you had judges entering the system who had actually grown up in such leased hovels, and who went without heat, running water, and proper toilet facilities as children, and never forgot it. You had judges in power who had little sympathy for the landlords' mantra of take it or leave it.

But even with a change in judicial outlook, there was still the conceptual problem of contract law standing in the way. If a landlord did not contractually agree to provide a habitable living space, how could you force him or her into it? Contract law reigned supreme in a common law court. Parties were free to agree to any arrangement, which included the lease of less than desirable premises. If habitability wasn't in the contract, a landlord didn't have to provide it. Meanwhile, the outbreaks of cholera, typhoid, and other maladies were eating away at urban areas.

Finally the new judges found a way around the contract problem. Instead of requiring that habitability be specifically stated as a contract term, they found that habitability was implied in every lease contract. It was a unique judicial turn and a triumph of public policy over contract law. Basically the courts began saying that if a landlord wouldn't specifically write habitability into a contract, then the court will imply that a warranty of habitability existed anyway.

Accordingly, it is implied that when a tenant leases a property that it be fit for human occupancy. The implied warranty gets to the heart of every lease transaction: Why would anyone live in a place that was unfit for human habitation?

And so in today's world, you, as the landlord, must manage and maintain your residential property in a manner that is acceptable for men, women, and children to live in. And when compared to the previous societal outbreaks of cholera, typhoid, plague, and hepatitis, this burden is no burden at all.

It should be noted that a landlord's duty to maintain, inspect, repair, and make habitable a property cannot be delegated to a property manager. While property managers have a duty to notify the landlord regarding their management and maintenance of the property, the landlord is ultimately responsible for all conditions of the property and is liable for the property manager's actions as well.

Given this discussion, clearly there is landlord liability when owning investment or rental real estate. As a landlord, your greatest risk will come when dangerous conditions are allowed to exist on the property. A list of these types of conditions would include (but not be limited to):

- Dangerous animals
- Unfinished repairs
- Broken fixtures
- Poorly maintained locks, doors, gates, lights, and safety measures
- Continuous criminal activity

Failure to correct a dangerous condition will result in potential landlord liability. Obviously, your first line of defense is to never allow such a condition to arise. Keep the property maintained and repaired. Provide your tenants with a decent place to live.

That said, however, in this world things can happen that no one would ever anticipate or foresee. And yet responsibility for such acts may rest squarely on your shoulders. You are the landlord. You are responsible. It's that simple. And that scary. So it is up to you to protect yourself.

There are two main ways of doing this: insurance and entity usage, which will be discussed in the following chapters.

Chapter 18

Insurance

Harmon and Chen

Harmon and Chen were friends and real estate investors. They owned four-unit apartment buildings next door to each other on Elm Street, in an older part of town. The neighborhood was a strong rental area because it was within walking distance of shopping areas and large downtown employers. The structures had been built over eighty years ago as large homes and had been remodeled into apartments as the neighborhood had changed.

While the Elm Street apartment buildings were almost the same, the strategies of their owners were quite different. Chen was a cautious and prudent individual, and always made sure his apartment buildings were well insured. Harmon used to kid Chen about enriching the insurance companies and Chen would take it in good humor. But Chen was convinced that insurance was his first line of defense and a limited liability entity to hold his property was his second line of defense. He wanted as much protection as possible. So he purchased a comprehensive commercial insurance package on the building. This included liability insurance, which covered injuries to third parties on the property. Chen knew if someone slipped and fell there would be a lawsuit and he wanted to be covered.

Chen had a workmen's compensation insurance policy so that if an employee was injured while working on the building there would be coverage. There was also a feature that covered the increased cost of construction so that if there were additional costs to bring new construction up to code, it would be covered. Furthermore, Chen's policy covered the loss of rents during an interruption or while any construction was occurring. On top of all this he obtained an umbrella override policy that provided another $2 million in higher limits for extra protection. And, for added extra protection, he held the property in a limited liability company instead of his own name.

As Chen was prudent, Harmon took risks. He owned rental properties all over town and had never had a problem. He didn't want to pay a lot of money for what he considered overpriced insurance coverage that would never be used, nor did he want to pay the initial and continuing fees for a limited liability entity. So he obtained the minimum possible fire and liability coverage and held the property in his own name.

One severely hot summer day, a mass of black clouds formed right over downtown and began crashing together. The result was the most jarring and frightening thunder and lightning storm the city had ever seen. Five bright white bolts of lightning cracked down onto Elm Street, touching off fires in both Chen's and Harmon's properties. In the tinderlike conditions, the two-story buildings were immediately engulfed in flames. By the time the fire department could respond, the buildings had burned to the basements and were completely gutted. While fortunately no one was killed in the conflagration, Chen's handyman employee broke his leg getting out. Worse yet, one of Harmon's tenants, MacArthur, broke his back when jumping from the second floor to escape the flames.

After everything settled down and the tenants were properly relocated, plans to rebuild were discussed. Chen was soon thankful to have enough insurance coverage. The city now required that any new construction be brought up to code. While the old buildings had been grandfathered in, a new apartment building would have to have a handicap access as well as be designed to accommodate expensive new flood abatement regulations. As the buildings were set low in a gully, the handicap access was going to be very expensive. Flood abatement measures in the gully were going to be more expensive still. But Chen had a comprehensive policy that covered any increased cost of construction. So the new and expensive additions, the new access and flood abatement requirements, were paid for by the insurance company.

Harmon was not so lucky. His coverage would replace whatever was lost—an older building that was not up to code. He would have to pay for the expensive upgrades himself.

Harmon received further bad news. His policy did not cover loss of rents, so while his tenants had moved out and the property generated no income, the mortgage payments were still due. The bank didn't really care if the property burned down and the tenants were gone. They just wanted the mortgage to be paid on time. If Harmon had to come out of pocket for it, that was his problem.

Chen, meanwhile, had a policy that covered loss of rents. His mortgage and other vendor payments were covered by a monthly payment he received from the insurance company. Chen was also covered by his workmen's compensation policy for the handyman with a broken leg. All expenses and claims were being covered.

On the other hand, most troubling for Harmon was the injured tenant. On a very personal level he was upset that MacArthur, with a broken back, had to be in so much pain and remain out of work for at least ten months. On a financial level, the injury was catastrophic as well. Harmon's policy level was not high enough to cover all of MacArthur's claims. There would certainly be a lawsuit. With the property held not in a limited liability company but in Harmon's name individually, MacArthur's attorneys were sure to seek recovery from Harmon's personal assets.

As it worked out, Chen had his plans approved by the city for an eight-unit apartment building. Harmon had been forced into bankruptcy and had to sell the Elm Street land. Chen was willing to help an old friend in need by buying Harmon's land in a transaction that made sense for Chen as well. Spreading out the cost of access and flood abatement over eight units instead of four made perfect sense. So did arranging for a sufficient amount of insurance on the new building.

As the case illustrates, like Harmon, you may think you'll never need insurance and may despise the idea of paying the premiums for something you think you'll never use. But when disaster hits you'll never be more pleased to be adequately insured. For many people, insurance is akin to carrying an umbrella on a cloudy day—if you carry one with you all day, it probably won't rain. If you don't bring your umbrella, however, it is sure to rain.

Insurance Broker

How to arrange for the right coverage is best handled by an experienced insurance broker. An individual with experience in handling claims and coverages as well as knowing the local market will be of great benefit to you.

An example of an experienced broker is John, a senior insurance executive in Napa, California. The city of Napa, located in the heart of California's renowned wine-making region, is one of the few municipalities in the country that requires all new single-family homes to be installed with interior fire-retarding sprinkler systems. It is a unique and expensive local requirement that only an experienced broker would know about and appreciate. As a result, John counsels his clients to consider coverage for an increased cost of construction in the event of damage. With the city of Napa requiring all new homes to have sprinkler systems, a policy providing only for replacement coverage—a home without sprinklers—will not best serve the owner. Indeed, a house may never get rebuilt due to the high additional expense a less than fully covered owner would have to personally pay for a sprinkler system.

John also recommends an often overlooked insurance for his clients known as non-owned and hired auto coverage. If you have an employee or property manager using their own car, for example, to make a deposit at the bank and they cause an accident, their primary auto coverage will come into play. However, if the plaintiff's attorney discovers that your property manager was on business for you, it is easy for you to be sued as well. The non-owned and hired auto coverage will cover your defense costs and claims in the suit, leaving you with a measure of peace of mind.

Another overlooked coverage John suggests considering is employment practices liability. If you have one or more employees in your real estate business you may be sued, like any other business owner, for wrongful termination, discriminatory actions, or sexual harassment. The workplace in today's society is filled with such claims and, whether bogus or legitimate, obtaining coverage against such trouble is essential.

In a related vein, insurance can be acquired to cover employee dishonesty. If your property manager or bookkeeper is handling a lot of money, insurance to cover the risk of embezzlement or theft may be worth reviewing.

The key in the area of insurance coverage is to bring the right insurance broker in at the start. Use the techniques we discussed in Chapter 2 on assembling your team. Make sure your team is knowledgeable and experienced and that each member is willing to be proactive on your behalf. You don't want someone who is content to simply collect premiums from you. Instead, you want a broker who is thinking about you and your properties in a way that is geared toward risk management and not fee enhancement.

Rich Dad Tip

The insurance industry, in the face of record claims, is now in the process of reconsidering coverage on certain properties. If a number of water damage, storm damage, burglary, or other claims have been filed against one property, insurance companies are now refusing to insure the property. Coverage is not based on the owner, who may have a spotless record, but on the property's history. As a potential buyer of the property, you need to know if it can be insured. Your bank will most likely not give you a loan if it can't.

The property's profile is found on an insurance industry database known as the Comprehensive Loss Underwriting Exchange, or CLUE. Since only the current property owner can order a CLUE report (online at www.choicetrust.com), buyers may want to require sellers to provide them with a clean and insurable CLUE report. A negative report may force owners to pay much higher premiums with a nonstandard carrier, such as Lloyds of London.

Chapter 19

Joint Tenancies/ Tenancies in Common/Land Trusts

How Not to Hold Real Estate

There is a misunderstood myth among the public that real estate protection is easily achieved through jointly owned or trustee-administered property. As with many misunderstood myths, the opposite is actually true. There is no asset protection at all when holding real estate as a joint tenant, tenant in common, or in a land trust. Indeed, in some cases you are even exposing yourself to a greater range of problems.

Calvin and Mariah

Calvin and Mariah were star-crossed lovers whose story would have made a great country and western ballad. It had all the elements: jail, betrayal, pickups, and misunderstood myths.

Calvin had met Mariah at Gilley's, near Houston, when it was the center of the mechanized bull-riding universe. Calvin could ride that bull for eons and Mariah just had to get to know him. Leaving in Calvin's Ford F-150 pickup truck, they took a ride to his duplex to get further acquainted. Calvin and Mariah hit it off and were soon spending a great deal of time together at the duplex.

Calvin was an alpaca farmer and was raising eight alpacas out back of the duplex so that America could wear fine wool sweaters. The alpaca promoters had said he would be rich in eighteen months. He was at month sixteen.

Mariah was quite interested in his future. So much so that she wanted to be a part of it. She began persuading him through the withholding of rewards that she should be more involved in his big future.

Calvin had heard through his friend Ronnie that if you held your property jointly with someone else a creditor couldn't get at your property. Calvin always had creditors looking for his money.

He could never qualify for a home loan so he had scraped enough money through various scofflaw schemes to own the duplex free and clear. But then he didn't have enough money to pay for the necessary property insurance and maintenance items the place needed. Calvin hadn't told Mariah that there were some credit issues, but she didn't need to know. Instead, he could get her off his back at the same time he was keeping the creditors at bay by putting her name on the duplex.

Calvin went to a stationery store to pick up a jointly owned property form. The high schooler with glazed eyes behind the counter asked if he wanted a tenants in common or joint tenant form. Calvin asked what worked best. The clerk laughed a little too loud and said the joint one, and so that was the one Calvin bought.

With the form all signed and recorded Calvin informed Mariah that she was now a joint tenant in the duplex. She was very happy. Just as they were about to celebrate they heard a blood-curdling scream from out back. Rushing to the scene they found Willie, the tenant in the duplex, with blood all over his hands. Willie screamed that the alpacas had attacked him and that Calvin was liable for keeping dangerous animals on the premises. Calvin laughed and said that he and Mariah were both liable. Mariah raised an eyebrow at this but Calvin continued to assert that because the property was held in a joint tenancy, Willie couldn't collect anything on any claim he could concoct. He told Willie to go wash his hands and quit bellyaching over a little nip on the hand.

Willie washed his hands and went to the personal injury lawyer on the cover of the phone book. Bo Jones was ecstatic to see that Willie had lost half of his pinkie finger and part of his ring finger. He promptly sued Calvin and Mariah as joint tenants of the duplex. The lawyer alleged that because the two of them had an equal undivided interest in the property as joint tenants, they were equally and personally responsible for the dangerous animals. Because Calvin had no insurance coverage, upon prevailing in front of a jury of their peers, Bo Jones was able to attach the jointly held interest, partition the property, and sell the duplex to satisfy the judgment Willie had against Calvin and Mariah. To compound their problems, shortly after Willie got bitten the county's animal control division took the alpacas and destroyed them, calling them a public nuisance, one month before Mariah expected their fortune to be made.

Mariah was not happy at this turn of events. She threatened to leave Calvin. But Calvin persuaded her to stay. He would do better the next time. To do so, he visited his friend Ronnie in jail. Calvin angrily told Ronnie how the jointly owned property format he said to use offered no asset protection at all. The darned attorney went right through the joint tenancy and snagged the duplex.

Ronnie laughed at him and told him he had used the wrong form. The joint tenancy was totally improper, Ronnie explained, because it allowed Mariah to own all of the property if Calvin died. It was called right of survivorship and it meant that she, as the surviving joint tenant after Calvin's demise, got to keep everything. Ronnie asked if Calvin wanted any of his seven kids from the first three marriages to get anything. Calvin did, and so Ronnie said that next time he had to use the tenants in common form. By having Mariah's name on it, his assets would be protected and Mariah would be satisfied. Calvin grumbled that there probably would never be a next time, since he had just lost everything.

Headed home, Calvin was stopped at a light listening to Tammy Wynette and lost in thought when a huge black Ford F-350 pickup rearended him at forty-five miles per hour. The driver hadn't even braked before impact, and Calvin's F-150 was totaled. Calvin suffered severe whiplash and was in great pain.

After months of intensive chiropractic and massage therapy, Calvin collected from the driver's insurance company. He and Mariah then bought another duplex and, as Ronnie had counseled, took title as tenants in common.

Mariah wanted Calvin to be more successful this time. Eight alpacas weren't going to get her to South Padre Island. Calvin had to make more money, plain and simple.

Calvin told Mariah of his plan to brew what he called Golden Mash. They could start out small, build a market for it, and then make some real money. The real money part was of interest to Mariah, so they began using the upstairs bathroom in the duplex as their distillery.

Soon their Golden Mash was finding a market in the local area among the young, hip, and very young. The still in the bathroom became crowded with equipment and tubing and gallon bottles filled with mash were stacked to the ceiling in the bathroom. The weight of all of this was eventually too much for the small room. The bathtub crashed through the ceiling into the apartment below, severely hurting Jimmie, the downstairs tenant.

As he was being loaded into the ambulance, Jimmie yelled at Calvin that he was liable for leasing out unsafe premises. Calvin laughed and said that he and Mariah were both liable but that because the property was held as tenants in common, no one was going to collect nothing.

Attorney Bo Jones was ecstatic to see that Jimmie was so badly injured. He promptly sued Calvin and Mariah as tenants in common in the duplex. Each owned a divided one-half interest in the property but they were collectively and personally responsible for Jimmie's injuries. Because Calvin had little insurance coverage, upon prevailing in front of a jury of their peers, Bo Jones was able to attach their divided tenancy in common interests and sell the duplex to satisfy the judgment Jimmie had against Calvin and Mariah. As well, the county authorities learned of the unlicensed distillery and slapped them with a fine and an order to never again engage in such an activity.

Mariah was not a happy person. She scolded Calvin for ever listening to jailbird Ronnie and his obviously incorrect ideas about jointly owned property. Ronnie had been incarcerated for practicing law without a license. Bo Jones had taken two duplexes away from them with ease, like a hot knife through lard. If they ever owned property again Mariah was going to a seminar to learn how to do it right.

A few days later Mariah was driving their new Ford F-150 pickup when she thought she saw a child chasing a ball into the street. Just to be safe she slammed on her brakes, causing a big Dodge Ram quad cab that was following too closely to slam into her. The Dodge totaled the pickup, and Mariah suffered extreme whiplash injury.

After months of highly intensive chiropractic and massage therapy, Mariah collected from the driver's insurance company. She and Calvin then bought another duplex. This time, having attended a free seminar given by a frail and excitable paralegal who sold expensive bundled form packages, she had the title to the duplex held in the name of a land trust. The paralegal said the land trust offered privacy and asset protection and, given their history, that was obviously what she and Calvin needed. For privacy protection the paralegal offered to serve as the trustee for $50 a year. For his money, the paralegal promised never to tell anyone anything. With his name on the deed as trustee, no one would really know who owned the duplex. That was good, thought Mariah, since every time their names were on the deed an attorney—and the same one at that—took the property away.

With their new duplex set up, Mariah informed Calvin that he needed to be more successful. This was their third duplex and she felt that she should be in a triplex by now. Mariah didn't want to do alpacas or mash or anything that took a lot of time. She wanted to try distributing a home remedy for depression. Her brother was doing it in Miami and making a huge amount of money from ordinary people who just wanted to feel good.

Soon, their home remedy for depression was finding a market in the local area among the young, hip, and very young. They were making a great deal of money and the duplex became known as the home remedy house.

The local prosecutor did not like home remedy houses. They were unlicensed and offered too great an opportunity for people to feel good. It had to be shut down. So the prosecutor had a police officer go in and pretend to want to feel good. Finally the sixth officer who went in was able to get out with the proper evidence against the home remedy for depression masterminds. The prosecutor obtained a warrant for the arrest of Calvin and Mariah. At a hearing, Calvin was asked if he owned the home remedy house. Thinking that the duplex was owned by the land trust and the $50 per year trustee, he said no. The prosecutor then called in the frail and excitable paralegal, who was frightened to the point of almost uncontrollable twitching. Without hesitation the paralegal testified that Calvin and Mariah were the beneficial owners of the home remedy house.

As the criminal case was nearing trial, Bo Jones, now on behalf of Calvin and Mariah, made an interesting legal discovery. It turned out that there were no laws on the books outlawing the sale of home remedies for depression. Congress and all of the states were quickly implementing such prohibitions but for now Calvin and Mariah hadn't broken any laws because there weren't any on the books to break.

The prosecutor had to let Mariah go. But he kept Calvin. A settlement was reached whereby Calvin got to join his friend Ronnie for six months. Calvin had committed perjury when he said he didn't own the duplex. He was the beneficial owner of the land trust that owned the duplex. To say he didn't own the duplex was a lie and he knew—or at least should have known—he was committing perjury.

For her part, Mariah got to keep the duplex. She spends her time driving carefully around the neighborhood.

As the case illustrates, there is no asset protection to be gained from holding real estate as jointly owned or land-trust-administered property. Still, because over three quarters of real estate owned by married couples in the United States is held in joint ownership, it is important to understand the concepts and consequences.

Tenancies in Common

The most common form of shared property ownership is the tenancy in common. Tenants in common each own a separate fractional share of the property, which a tenant in common may freely sell, encumber, bequeath by will or trust, or otherwise transfer. Unlike a joint tenancy, a tenant in common's sale of their share of the property will not change the nature of the tenancy. The purchaser or heir of an interest in a tenancy in common receives the same rights and privileges as the former tenant.

Each tenant in common has the right to benefit from the property. This includes the rights to use the property, exclude third parties from it, and receive a portion of any income produced from it. Legal remedies are available to tenants in common to enforce their fractional rights to the property. These include remedies that allow the property to be physically divided, divided by sale, or for tenants to demand an accounting and payment corresponding to their interest in the property. However, other forms of shared property ownership may provide desirable features that are not present in a tenancy in common.

Joint Tenancies

Joint tenancies were once, and still are in some states, a prominent form of shared property ownership. When two or more persons clearly agree in writing to hold real estate in equal and undivided shares, a joint tenancy may be created. Most states prefer tenancies in common, so any agreement attempting to create a joint tenancy should clearly state that a joint tenancy with survivorship, and not a tenancy in common, is being created. Joint tenancies are popular among married couples because joint tenancies uniquely provide for an undivided interest and survivorship.

During the life of joint tenants, each joint tenant owns the entire property. However, each joint tenant has equal rights to use and occupy all of the property. Unlike a tenant in common's divided and separate property interest, a joint tenant's interest is undivided. A joint tenant cannot sell his or her interest in the tenancy without severing the joint tenancy and creating a tenancy in common. In severing the joint tenancy, a joint tenant removes the unique features of undivided interest and survivorship.

While the conversion of the undivided interest to a divided interest in the severing of a joint tenancy has little practical effect, the removal of the feature of survivorship is detrimental to other joint tenants. Survivorship provides joint tenants rights that differ from those enjoyed by tenants in common. A tenant in common may bequeath their interest through a will or trust or their interest may be transferred to an heir by operation of law. Joint tenants cannot bequeath their joint tenancy interest. Upon the death of a joint tenant, the surviving tenant(s) automatically own the entire property by operation of law. The property interest held by the deceased joint tenant simply ceases to exist, leaving the surviving joint tenant(s) with the entire interest in the property. This automatic transfer feature is called a right of survivorship. If a joint tenancy is severed, the surviving joint tenant(s) is (are) denied the right of survivorship.

The right of survivorship is the reason why married couples often use joint tenancies. If a married couple use a tenancy in common and each spouse does not provide for the transfer of their tenancy interest in a will or trust, default rules of inheritance will apply through what is known as intestate succession. Intestate succession does not always provide the result the joint tenants would have wanted. Furthermore, the deceased spouse's property interest must go through probate if it is handled under intestate succession or through the administration of a will. By holding property as joint tenants with right of survivorship, commonly abbreviated as JTWROS, married couples know how each spouse's property interest will be treated upon the other's death. If one spouse unexpectedly passes away, the real estate automatically will transfer to the survivor by operation of law. This may allow the surviving spouse to use or sell the property without waiting for the property interest to go through probate.

An example helps to explain the difference between a joint tenancy and a tenancy in common. David and Michelle own a speedboat together. If they own it as joint tenants, they have an undivided interest and a right of survivorship for the whole boat. David doesn't own the engine and Michelle doesn't own the steering wheel. Instead, together they own the whole boat, bow to stern, equally in an undivided fashion. The boat is an indivisible unit of property. Upon the death of either David or Michelle, the survivor will automatically own the entire boat. On the other hand, if they own the boat equally as tenants in common, David and Michelle own specific and divided interests in the boat. Much like a corporation, they own a separate 50 percent interest in the boat and, again like a corporation, they can sell their half-interest to whomever they want without affecting each other's interests. While they still don't own the engine or the steering wheel separately, as tenants in common, they own and are able to sell a set percentage interest in the boat. Upon the death of either David or Michelle, the deceased's tenancy in common interest may be distributed pursuant to a will, trust, or intestate succession.

Tenancies by the Entirety

A tenancy by the entirety is a unique form of shared property ownership that can exist only between married persons. Tenancies by the entirety are increasingly rare, but are used by spouses in some states in the same manner as joint tenancies. Like joint tenancies, tenancies by the entirety create an undivided interest and provide a right of survivorship. However, unlike joint tenancies, tenancies by the entirety could not traditionally be severed by the unilateral act of one tenant.

Tenancies by the entirety, like all property interests, hark back to old English law and custom. Tenancies by the entirety were originally based on sexist notions of property ownership. A married man and woman were treated as a unification of two people. Their property was treated as being owned by the unity or the "entirety" of the two, and not as being owned by two separate individuals. Under the modern joint tenancy, a husband can sever the tenancy and remove his wife's right of survivorship by selling his interest in the property. Under the traditional tenancy by the entirety, a husband could not sever the tenancy, but could only sell his right to use the property during his lifetime and his right of survivorship. This retained a right of survivorship for his wife, thus protecting her financial interests as a widow.

Modern treatment of tenancies by the entirety varies among the states. Contemporary notions of sexual equality remove the paternalistic basis for tenancies by the entirety. However, some states have retained tenancies by the entirety, because they believe that tenancies by the entirety serve an additional function. Because tenancies by the entirety traditionally prevented a husband from conveying his wife's right of survivorship, they also prevented creditors from seizing the couple's property based on financial obligations of one spouse. This function of tenancies by the entirety may allow couples in certain states to use tenancies by the entirety to protect their assets; however, a recent United States Supreme Court decision indicates that tenancies by the entirety will not protect against federal taxes. See *U.S. v. Craft*, 122 S. Ct. 1414 (2002). Because states treat tenancies by the entirety differently, and because they may not provide complete asset protection, you should consult with your local advisor before proceeding with transactions involving tenancies by the entirety.

Protection and Title

As we saw in our last case, jointly held property—be it in a joint tenancy or as tenants in common—does not limit your liability as an owner of real estate.

With a tenancy in common, a creditor can obtain a court order to sell the property to satisfy a judgment. In Calvin and Mariah's case, the property was sold to pay for a claim against the property owners. But what if one of the co-tenants has a claim against him or her for a problem that is totally unrelated to the property? The property interest may still be sold. As such, you may be an innocent co-tenant and find yourself owning the property with an entirely new person, who may not be to your liking, and may not share your view of how to manage and benefit from the property. If you must use a tenancy in common, do all that you can to be sure that your co-tenants are free from current or future financial problems.

While property held as a joint tenant cannot be seized as easily as that of a tenant in common, there is still no asset protection involved. Creditors of a joint tenant can obtain a court order to partition the property, thus converting the ownership to that of tenants in common, and then sell the property to satisfy their claim.

As well, land trusts do not offer asset protection either. What they do quite well is offer privacy. This is because title is recorded in the name of the trustee of the land trust, not in the name(s) of the beneficiaries—or true owners—of the trust. A potential claimant may do a title search of property held in your name and not find anything, since it is all recorded in the names of unrelated trustees. The fact that a search does not turn up any ready assets to proceed against may well deter litigation.

However, once sued, a land trust will not protect you from liability. If a tenant is injured on property in which you are the personal beneficiary of a land trust, you will be personally responsible. If a claim unrelated to the property arises and a creditor is seeking assets to satisfy a judgment, your beneficial ownership in a land trust may be reached. And if you are asked in court if you have any interests in real estate, you must disclose that you own a beneficial interest in a land trust.

That said, there is good news to report. In foreshadowing the next section on how to hold real estate, having a land trust be beneficially owned by a limited liability company (LLC) is an excellent strategy. The land trust offers superb privacy and the LLC offers asset protection.

Use of a land trust is not without certain practical considerations. When seeking financing, many trustees will not be too willing to sign any mortgage documents, fearing personal liability for the obligation. Frequently, title must be placed in the owner's individual name for recording of the mortgage. As well, because a land trust is an interest in personal property, Section 1031 like-kind, tax-free exchanges will not be available since only the exchange of real property is allowed. Again, title will have to be transferred out of the land trust for an exchange to work. Of course, in both cases, transferring the title compromises the privacy that was sought in the first place.

Nevertheless, as mentioned, in the right circumstances a land trust beneficially owned by an LLC can be a winning combination.

Chapter 20

How to Hold Real Estate

From a legal and tax standpoint, limited liability companies (LLCs) and limited partnerships (LPs) offer the greatest protection for holding real estate.

The best way to appreciate these advantages is to compare LLCs and LPs with other entities and means of holding real estate. First, we'll review two tables that spell out the differences. Then we'll consider several cases that further help illustrate the distinguishing features.*

The first table details the language of the entities we shall consider. While the structural elements are similar, the terminology is different and must be appreciated.

The second table is a comparison of the corporate structure of the various types of entities we will be discussing.

As we go through our next three cases, some of the practical differences between entities will become apparent.

*Additional discussions of entity differences can be found in *Own Your Own Corporation* (Warner Books) and *How to Use Limited Liability Companies and Limited Partnerships* (Success DNA), both by Garrett Sutton. Both books may be obtained at www.successdna.com.

The Language of Entities

Term	LLC (Limited Liability Company)	LP (Limited Partnership)	Corporation
Owner	Member	General and Limited Partner	Shareholder
Ownership Interests	Membership Interest	Partnership Interest	Shares of Stock
Initial Filing Document (filed with Secretary of State)	Articles of Organization	Certificate of Limited Partnership (LP-1)	Articles of Incorporation
Organizational Document	Operating Agreement	Limited Partnership Agreement	Bylaws
Management	Manager	General Partner	Chairman of the Board; Chief Executive Officer; President

Moe

Moe was a coot. He was set in his ways, to the point of fossilization. New ideas were the enemy. Advice was not sought or welcomed. Moe ran an auto repair shop as a sole proprietor. Moe adamantly ignored meek attempts at advice from his friends, family, and bookkeeper that he operate as a corporation to limit his liability. Moe had operated as a sole proprietor for twenty years and had never been sued. That was enough for him. Why spend a few hundred extra dollars a year for protection he didn't need? Corporations were just a scheme by attorneys and accountants to sell their services.

So Moe continued just as he pleased, fixing Fords and Chevys in his old, rented brick garage on the south side of town.

Recently, Tommy the landlord had come to Moe with a proposition. Tommy was retiring and moving to the San Juan Islands, and was selling his real estate holdings around town. Moe had always paid the rent on time, and Tommy appreciated that. Tommy felt a kinship to his laconic, unchanging tenant and wanted Moe to have the first chance to buy the building.

For once, Moe was willing to consider a new idea—owning his own building. Of course, with the rent he had expended every month he could have bought and paid for his own garage years ago, but Moe was not secure

Corporate Structure of Entities

	C Corporation	S Corporation	LLC (Limited Liability Company)	LP (Limited Partnership)	General Partnership	Sole Proprietorship
Personal liability for business debts?	No personal liability of shareholders	No personal liability of shareholders	No personal liability of members	General partner(s) personally liable; limited partners not personally liable	General partners personally liable	Sole proprietor personally liable
Who can legally obligate the business?	Officers and directors	Officers and directors	In member-managed, any member. In manager-managed, any manager	Any general partner, not limited partners	Any general partner	Sole proprietor
Responsibility for management decisions	Board of directors, officers	Board of directors, officers	Same as above	Same as above	General partners	Sole proprietor
Ownership restrictions	Most states allow one-shareholder corporations; some require at least two	No more than 75 shareholders allowed; no foreign entities or individuals or domestic entities allowed	Most states allow one-member LLCs	One general partner and one limited partner required	At least two general partners	Only one sole proprietor and no more
Start-up and ongoing formalities	Articles filed with state; bylaws and annual meetings required	Articles filed with state; Form 2553 filed with IRS; bylaws and annual meetings required	Articles filed with state; operating agreement and annual meetings not required, but strongly recommended	LP-1 filed with state; partnership agreement and annual meeting not required, but recommended	No state filing; partnership agreement recommended; no meetings required	No state filing, no meetings required
Limits on transferability of interests	Transfers may be limited by agreement or by securities laws	Transfers may be limited by agreement or by securities laws; transfers to nonqualified persons may cause loss of S corporation status	Unanimous or super-majority consent may be required by non-transferring members	Consent of all partners may be required	Consent of all partners may be required	Can sell business to another
Business effect on death or departure of owner	Corporation continues	Corporation continues	In some states, dissolution unless members vote to continue	Automatic dissolution unless provided for in partnership agreement	Automatic dissolution unless provided for in partnership agreement	Automatic dissolution
Taxation of business profits	Corporate profits taxed at corporate rates; dividends taxed at individual rates of shareholders	Individual tax rates of shareholders	Individual tax rates of members unless LLC elects corporate taxation	Individual tax rates of general and limited partners	Individual tax rates of general partners	Individual tax rate of sole proprietor

in his business then, and he liked having Tommy take care of the ownership matters. Paying rent was okay. But now Tommy was telling Moe that he didn't know who would buy the building if Moe didn't. A new landlord could raise the rent, or worse yet, evict Moe from the space he'd been comfortable in and used for twenty years. That was enough for Moe. He wanted to own the garage to prevent someone else from fooling with his familiar surroundings.

An agreement was quickly reached and a loan to purchase the garage duly arranged. Prior to closing, Moe met with Tommy and the loan officer. The issue of how title to the property was to be held came up. Moe wasn't even aware that it was an issue. The property was his—wouldn't he hold it in his name automatically?

Tommy explained that there were many ways to hold title to the property. There was joint tenancy, tenancy in common, and other shared ownership methods. There were also ways for a sole business owner like himself to own property, primarily by using a limited liability company or, if he wanted to take a few extra steps, by using a limited partnership. Tommy noted that such an entity, if properly set up, could protect Moe into the future.

To both Tommy's and the loan officer's surprise, Moe would have none of it. He became quite angry, and said that he was a sole proprietor, and wasn't going to pay for any extra services he didn't need. Tommy calmly tried to explain the advantages to Moe but the concepts of limited liability and asset protection only inflamed Moe's positions about the uselessness and outrageous expense of professional services even more.

Tommy calmed Moe down. He was worried that the loan officer would question Moe's stability and would deny the loan. Tommy had tried to help Moe and couldn't—so he let it go. If Moe wanted to own the old brick garage in his name personally, that was Moe's decision.

The transaction went through. Moe had put $50,000 down on the $150,000 property. The $100,000 loan was made personally to Moe and the property was held in Moe's name as an individual. The $50,000 down payment represented a great deal of Moe's total net worth, but Moe felt it was worth the investment to keep his familiar surroundings the same.

And then the inevitable happened. Moe was sued for negligence in a car repair he had performed. The Toyota's owner had driven from the old brick garage straight into a store across the street. The steering had failed. The injuries to the driver and her family member passenger were significant. The medical bills were huge. Moe's insurance policy did not adequately cover him for claims due to negligent work.

Soon a lawsuit was filed, and in short order a huge money judgment was rendered against Moe. Moe was left totally exposed to the claim.

By doing business as a sole proprietorship he had no protection whatsoever from this judgment. His house, bank account, and personal assets were free for the creditor to reach. As well, by holding the old brick garage in his own name, the building in which he had a $50,000 equity interest in was also exposed.

In a matter of months the attorneys for the injured family reached all of Moe's assets, including the old brick garage. Had Moe listened to Tommy's advice, the building could have been protected with an LLC. If he had listened to the advice of his friends, family, and bookkeeper, his business could have been protected with a corporation.

But, as we know, Moe didn't listen to, or even want, advice. Instead, he actively refused advice. And, as a consequence, he lost everything and soon thereafter died destitute.

The lesson of Moe's case is twofold. First, be open to the advice of others. You don't always need to follow it. But at least listen to it. Robert Kiyosaki's rich dad has taught that business and investing are team sports. By surrounding yourself with the right team of advisors you will come up with the right answers to the right questions. And with the correct strategies, many of which you are learning about now, you are going to be protected from the start and for the future.

Second, for maximum protection, consider holding your real estate in a protected entity. By holding property in your individual name you are inviting attack. By holding it in a properly structured and protected entity you are discouraging attack. That alone may give you a better night's sleep.

One point should be made here regarding borrowing money to purchase investment (or personal) real estate. There are many instances where a bank or mortgage company will require (1) the loan to be personally guaranteed by you, and (2) title to vest (be taken) in your individual name. Of course, if your LLC owns enough properties and has a strong enough financial statement, the bank may lend to the LLC without a personal guarantee. This is not likely to be the case at the beginning, when you first start buying properties. And it may never be the case if your strategy (and it is a good one) is to segregate assets and hold only one or a few properties in each LLC. So, be prepared for the requirement of an individual guarantee for the loan and title being vested in your individual name.

Many have complained that they want their real estate in a protected entity but the bank won't allow it. Fear not, because since you are wisely reading this book, you are going to learn some strategies and tricks to protect yourself.

First, as long as the bank has your personal guarantee, they are covered. If you default on the loan they are coming after you personally, no matter whose name the title is in. Having you guarantee the loan and have title in your own name is a measure of extra protection that banks and lenders are noted for. It is called a "belt and suspenders" strategy, which means using two types of support so that no one gets caught with their pants down.

But once your title has vested into your name, once you are listed on the public record as an owner, the bank is usually a little less concerned. It is at this point (or even before you sign the loan papers) that you tell the bank that for "estate planning" purposes you need the title to be vested in the name of an LLC or LP. These are the magic words that you need to use—"estate planning." Explain that to accomplish your estate plan gifting needs, to gift away your estate at a discount, you need your real estate to be owned by an LLC or an LP.* Most banks will understand this. They appreciate that many of their customers are sophisticated individuals with estate planning goals and issues that must be accomplished. They will appreciate that you are one of these individuals. And what will happen is that they will be okay with your estate planning goals and will approve of you filing a quit claim deed with the county recorder transferring title from your own name to the name of your LLC.

Of course, transferring title has its costs. There can be transfer and other taxes to be paid, as well as recording and document fees. If possible, it is preferable and cheaper to take title in the name of your LLC or LP at the start. If the bank won't allow it, by all means convince them with the estate planning argument that the transfer is appropriate shortly after title vests in your name. And transfer title within days of taking it in your own name. The

*Gifting LLC and LP interests at a discount is discussed in *How to Use Limited Liability Companies and Limited Partnerships* (SuccessDNA).

longer it is in your own name, the longer you are exposed to the risks Moe faced in our last case.

What are the consequences to the parties borrowing money to purchase real estate in your own name, taking title in your own name, and shortly thereafter transferring title to your LLC or LP? They are as follows:

1. *The Bank/Lender:* The bank has your personal guarantee for the loan. If you default on the loan, they can, subject to each state's law, go after you, the property, or both, for repayment. The bank is protected.

2. *Current and Future Creditors:* As long as property is in your individual name, current creditors can reach your personal assets. Once your property is transferred into an LLC or an LP, current creditors will still have a claim against you as an individual, because their claims arose when the property was held by you. But future creditors will only have a claim against the LLC or LP. And that's the protected space you want to be in.

3. *The Borrower:* You have personally guaranteed the loan. You will always be personally responsible for its repayment. But by transferring title to your protected entity, whatever claims come up against your property will be encapsulated in a limited liability entity. But remember, if you sign any contracts for the property in your personal name, you can still be held responsible. Be sure to sign as a manager of an LLC or a corporate general partner of an LP to avoid personal liability.

If you follow these simple formalities your personal assets will be shielded from attack. And that is the key here: While owing the bank some money is one thing, protecting yourself from the public is quite another. You know what you owe the bank. They are letting you use their money to grow your wealth. It's almost only fair that you give them a personal guarantee. But you have no idea what can happen with the public. There is no way to anticipate or prepare for what the public may deal you. And for that reason you need protection.

Now let's look at our next case, involving the use of another protected company—the corporation.

Jeffrey

Jeffrey had a thriving business going. He was the sole owner of two doughnut shops in two great, high-traffic locations. Jeffrey had a conscious strategy of hiring attractive young women from the local college to work in his shops. He had them wear short French maid outfits and promoted flirting with the customers. The male morning commuters loved coming into the store. So did Jeffrey. He took advantage of his strategy on several occasions. While he'd been slapped down a few times, he had also dated the help to his satisfaction.

In the last two years sales had been very good. Jeffrey, being a shrewd and fairly stubborn businessman, made sure that profits were very strong. He had incorporated his doughnut business as an S corporation, Jeffrey's Doughnuts, Inc., and cash was flowing through to him at a healthy rate. He now had some after-tax dollars to invest in real estate.

Jeffrey decided that he was going to buy two properties. The first property was a commercial building that he would use for his third doughnut shop. He liked the idea of being an owner-user, of paying himself rent instead of enriching another landlord. The second piece of property was a four-plex in an older part of town. It had a strong rental history and was in decent condition. Jeffrey liked the idea of receiving passive income from these investments.

However, Jeffrey had a blind spot when it came to segregating assets. He was penny wise and pound foolish, and felt that if one corporation provided asset protection, why would anyone need additional protected entities?

Jeffrey's accountant had suggested that the real estate should be held in two separate LLCs. One would hold the commercial building and another the four-plex. In this way, if a tenant at the four-plex sued over some issue, the commercial building was insulated from attack. Jeffrey couldn't grasp the concept and thought only that the accountant was giving this advice because he wanted to prepare and charge for two extra tax returns each year.

The accountant then suggested that at the very least both properties should be held in one LLC, separate and apart from the S corporation. In this way, if Jeffrey's Doughnuts, Inc. was sued for whatever reason, the real estate would be segregated away from reach in a separate, protected LLC.

But Jeffrey still thought the accountant was giving this advice because he wanted to prepare and charge for one extra tax return each year. He switched accountants and took title to both properties in his S corporation. Jeffrey's Doughnuts, Inc. now owned and operated three retail doughnut shops, and also owned one commercial building housing his third doughnut shop and one rental four-plex.

The beginning of the end came when Jeffrey was sued by five co-eds for sexual harassment. A jury of his peers decided that Jeffrey deliberately promoted a sexually charged and harassing workplace and found that the five women were entitled to a great deal of money. The co-eds' attorneys began proceedings to acquire Jeffrey's only real estate asset—the shares of the S corporation. Jeffrey was livid. How, he demanded of his own attorneys, could they reach the shares of a protected entity?

Quite simply, explained his attorneys. The lawsuit wasn't against Jeffrey's Doughnuts, Inc. If it had been, Jeffrey's personal assets would have been protected. Instead, the judgment was rendered against Jeffrey himself, as an individual, for it was his individual conduct that was determined to be wrongful. As such, all of his personal assets were exposed, including his shares in Jeffrey's Doughnuts, Inc. Jeffrey's attorneys then explained that by controlling all of the shares of Jeffrey's Doughnuts, Inc., the co-eds controlled all of the real estate in the corporation. They could hold a meeting and vote to sell the commercial building and four-plex to satisfy their claims. His attorneys also explained that if the real estate had been in an LLC or an LP he would have had a much better shot at protecting the property through the charging order procedure. This is a court order giving a creditor the right to receive a judgment debtor's distributions from an LLC or LP. It does not give the creditor voting rights, however, or a means to sell the assets, thus providing significant asset protection.

Jeffrey was furious at his previous accountant. How could he let him put all of the real estate into one corporation? Jeffrey called the accountant, shouted out his failings, and demanded that the properties be immediately transferred into a separate LLC. But his accountant knew the law. With great satisfaction the accountant informed Jeffrey that to transfer the properties now, with a judgment already rendered, would be considered a fraudulent conveyance, a transfer designed to defraud creditors. He explained that it was too late to make such a transfer, that to do so now would only cause more trouble for Jeffrey. He closed their conversation by telling him that he didn't want to work with Jeffrey anymore anyway, and hung up.

As it turned out, Jeffrey lost everything. With control of the shares of Jeffrey's Doughnuts, Inc., the co-eds sold all of the company's assets—the doughnut stores and the properties. Jeffrey never owned real estate again.

As important as knowing that protected entities should be used to hold real estate is knowing which protected entities not to use. As Jeffrey's case illustrates, just because a corporation offers limited liability does not mean it is the right entity for holding real estate. A judgment creditor of a corporation's shareholder can reach those shares and vote them to their own advantage. As we'll see in our next case, this is not the case with members of an LLC or limited partners in an LP. So, the lack of individual protection for corporate shares, when combined with the corporate tax treatment for real estate holdings Diane has discussed, provides a pretty persuasive argument against holding real estate in a corporation.

While Moe and Jeffrey did not fare well in their real estate investing, let's review a case where the owner did it right.

George

George was an avid outdoorsman, and particularly enjoyed exploring the jungles of Borneo. He had a remote tree house in Borneo where he lived for much of the year, returning to the United States at the beginning of Superbowl Week and staying to the end of Mardi Gras.

In order to finance his lifestyle George had made some very canny real estate investments during his previous life as a postal worker. Being on foot delivering mail, he was able to watch neighborhoods around him change and grow, and soon came to realize when a neighborhood was about to move upscale. George had bought his first three properties in neighborhoods like these, and had converted three large Victorian-style houses into a total of twelve apartments, which were always rented, and earned top rental dollars. George had also used a portion of his real estate income to purchase a fourth property, a section of undeveloped Florida swampland he had bought with the idea of building another tree house, for his stays in the United States. He affectionately referred to that land as "George's Jungle," and had a few "George's Jungle" and "Private—No Trespassing" signs put in various places around that property.

George had wanted his business to run as smoothly as possible, as he spent most of his time outside the country. He read many books, and consulted with a knowledgeable attorney and CPA about the best way to hold all of his properties. His first step had been to form three separate LLC entities, one to hold the title of each of his three apartment properties. His second step was to make sure that each LLC had its own tax ID number, a separate bank account, and that yearly entity records were prepared.

George understood that by keeping his assets segregated he was lessening the risk of all of his assets being attacked by a judgment creditor. And, as George was operating real estate rental property, he expected that sooner or later a tenant would make some type of claim. George also understood that by observing all of the required entity formalities, he was building up a strong defense to any attempts by a creditor to "pierce the corporate or LLC veil" and attack George personally. By keeping his businesses up to date, with separate bank accounts and annual entity records, George was establishing that each LLC existed as a separate and unique entity, rather than being just an offshoot of George himself.

Although he didn't relish the idea of operating a separate LLC for each apartment, he did decide that the risk would be manageable on a per-building basis. Each building had a mortgage over it, and each mortgage was in the name of its respective LLC. The banks had required George to sign personal guarantees over all three mortgages. But for all the other contracts involving the properties George had signed in his capacity as manager of each LLC. In this fashion, he was able to again add a layer of protection for himself personally and establish the separate formal existence of each LLC. However, George was also aware that if he defaulted on any of the mortgages it would wind up costing him personally, as he was the ultimate guarantor.

George was worried that he may be found personally liable for one risk or another. But all of George's LLC entities had been formed in Nevada, so that George could take advantage of Nevada's charging order procedure to deflect a potential personal judgment against him. George knew that the charging order was the only way a judgment creditor could attach a personal judgment to a property held by a Nevada LLC, and that the charging order would prevent the judgment creditor from interfering in the day-to-day operations of the apartment properties, or from attempting to force George into selling one of the properties to satisfy a claim. George's attorney had said that some courts outside Nevada may want to use their own charging order procedure if the land was located in their state, but George felt that there was a chance he could fight that. Would Nevada trump Florida? Only a judge could decide. Still, at the very least, by using Nevada LLCs to hold the property, he had the argument that Nevada's charging order procedure should apply.

The charging order procedure meant that the judgment creditor would have to sit as a "silent member" of sorts in the LLC, and receive distributions of profit if (and when) George decided to make them. George was the sole manager of each LLC, and under Nevada law, a manager alone has the right to decide to make profit distributions from an LLC. Nor could a judgment creditor attempt to vote George out at the LLC's annual meeting, because their status under the charging order did not come with voting rights—only the right to receive a distribution of the LLC's profits if—and when—the manager decided to make any. Better still, George knew, was that even though he would have to distribute some profits from each of the LLCs in order to finance his own lifestyle, any profits distributed to a judgment creditor would be treated by the IRS as income to that judgment creditor and taxed accordingly. Even better than that, George knew that if an LLC earned a profit, but the profit was invested back into the LLC, and not distributed to its members, then those members would wind up being assessed for tax on their portion of profits, even though they didn't receive a penny in their pockets! Known as phantom income, George liked that idea best of all. If someone were bound and determined to try and take his money, he reasoned, they should have to pay a price for that privilege. Coming out of pocket and paying the IRS in order to collect on a judgment is not a favored position for creditors.

George had formed a fourth LLC to manage his last property, the Florida swampland. Even though it wasn't developed, he knew enough to know that a few "Keep Out" signs would probably not be enough to absolve him of all liability if someone should be injured while trespassing. And there was no way that George wanted to expose himself personally to liability by holding title to that property in his own name.

The apartments were earning money hand over fist, property values were continuing to appreciate in each of the three neighborhoods, and everything was swinging George's way when the sadly inevitable happened—a group of teenagers out for some fun had gone onto George's swampland property to have a bush party. In fact, they had used many of George's "Private—No Trespassing" signs to start a large bonfire to better see their way in the dark jungle. Fortunately, the land was too damp for the bonfire to get out of control. Unfortunately, several teenagers had decided to go for a swim in an adjacent swimming hole, and the light from the bonfire had not, apparently, been enough to illuminate the waiting alligators. Given the situation, George felt it was somewhat lucky that only one young man had been mauled, and the rest of the swimming teens had managed to make it out of the water intact.

A lawsuit was launched against the LLC holding the Florida property, as well as George personally, in his capacity as manager of the LLC. George was concerned at being named personally, and about possibly losing control of all his hard-earned asset properties, but his attorney told him not to worry. As long has he had obeyed the entity formalities, his lawyer advised him, and had not done anything fraudulent or improper in his capacity as manager of the LLC, it would be very difficult for a court to find him personally liable. And, even if the worst happened, and George was found personally liable, his other properties were also held in LLCs, and George had obeyed required entity formalities for those entities as well. The best that a judgment creditor could hope to do would be to attach a charging order against George's interests in the other LLCs. While this would entitle a judgment creditor to a portion of the profits distributed to George from these other entities, it did not convey voting rights, or a right to force George into selling his interests in the other LLCs to satisfy a judgment against him. George was relieved.

At the trial, despite the fact that the teenagers were clearly trespassing on signed and marked private property, and the assertion by George's lawyer that the teenagers must have been aware of their trespass by their actions of using his signs as kindling for their fire, the jury still felt sympathy toward the unfortunate teen's family. A ruling in favor of the family was made, and a hefty sum of damages was awarded. However, the court found that George was not personally liable. The LLC's records clearly indicated that it had a distinct and separate existence, apart from George personally, and that George had done nothing wrong in his conduct as manager of the LLC. Therefore, as the court was unable to attach any liability to George himself, the ruling was made against George's LLC only.

As a result, the family had a claim against the assets of the LLC, the swampland. Since the LLC did not have any insurance coverage the court ordered that the land be sold to satisfy the claim. The only asset of the LLC was worth less than $10,000. The sale did not trouble George too much. The property taxes were a nuisance and the land wasn't appreciating. There was plenty more like it to be purchased at a later date.

With the exception of losing the swampland, George came through the entire ordeal in great shape. As he wasn't found to be personally liable, his personal assets (which included his interests in the other three LLCs holding the apartment properties) were safe from attack. He continued to receive flow-through distributions from his high-income properties, did some re-provisioning of supplies, and returned to the jungles of Borneo, where no one would dare sue for injuries incurred while trespassing.

The lesson of this case is that an LLC can offer superb asset protection. It is an excellent and recommended entity for holding real estate. It is a flexible entity allowing for great structuring opportunities.

In this regard, remember our discussion on whether Nevada would trump Florida? The issue was whether the charging order rules of Florida, because George's real estate was located there, would supersede the charging order rules of Nevada, the home state of the LLC. Among attorneys this is called a conflict (or choice) of laws issue. Which law applies: Nevada or Florida? A judge gets to choose.

In many states, especially where local real estate is involved, the local state law will apply. Knowing that, how can you protect yourself?

Let's use a New York example. The laws in the state of New York do not offer strong charging order protection. One would certainly use a Nevada LLC over a New York LLC if asset protection was the goal. However, if the real estate is located in New York there is a good chance that New York's weak charging order law would apply.

In that case, utilizing the LLC's flexible structuring features you may want to consider the following:

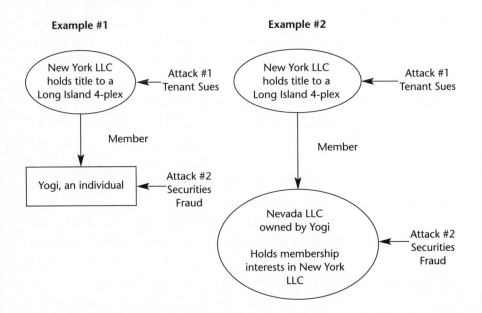

As with any structure, if a tenant in the Long Island four-plex fell, was injured, and sued as in Attack #1, absent proper insurance coverage the New York LLC would be responsible for any judgment. The New York LLC member, whether it is Yogi in Example #1 or Yogi's LLC in Example #2 should be protected from such a claim.

The issue arises when Yogi gets sued for something completely unrelated to the Long Island four-plex. Let's assume he gets sued for securities fraud as in Attack #2 and a judgment is entered against him. In Example #1, given New York's weak LLC asset protection laws, a judgment credit or could reach his membership interests in the New York LLC and force a sale of the property.

In Example #2 Yogi has much greater protection. With a Nevada LLC passively holding membership interests in a New York LLC there is a much stronger argument that Nevada's superior charging order laws must apply. The Nevada LLC does not hold New York real estate or avail itself of New York's legal system. Instead, all of its limited activities occur within the state of Nevada. If a creditor wants to reach Yogi's membership interests in the Nevada LLC he or she will have to utilize the Nevada courts and fight to obtain a less than desirable (from a creditor's viewpoint) charging order.

The point is that if you hold real estate in a state with weak or nonexistent charging order remedies, you may want to consider using two LLCs for protection. As in our example, the first local LLC holds the local real estate and the second Nevada LLC holds the membership interests in the first LLC. In this way, superior protection is obtained and maintained.

Chapter 21

Structures for Your Real Estate/ Tax Considerations

Chapter 20 discussed some of the legal considerations for structures you use to hold your property. There are also some tax considerations. First, though, it is helpful to review the types of business structures possible and the tax considerations.

There are four ways that you can be taxed on your property. These are:

1. S corporation
2. C corporation
3. partnership
4. personally held

S Corporation

The S corporation is a flow-through entity. The taxable income earned in the S corporation will flow through to the individual owners and be taxed at their individual rates. Distributions of an S corporation to the individual shareholder owners are done at fair market value. This can be a problem, as we'll see later.

The S corporation's main advantage over partnership taxation is that the earnings are not subject to self-employment tax. However, real estate passive income is not subject to self-employment tax, so there would be no S corporation benefit. Normally, an entity with partnership law is better for real estate holdings.

If your real estate business consists of flipping property, then the income could be considered active trade or business and thus subject to self-employment tax. In this case, an S corporation might make more sense.

C Corporation

A C corporation might make sense for real estate investing if there is foreign ownership of the corporation or if the company is publicly traded. Other than that, the C corporation is not a good choice for holding real estate. This is because the capital gains rate for the corporate level is much higher than for that of the individual rate. A flow-through entity such as a partnership would pay much lower taxes, provided the individual owners of the partnership *are* individuals.

Personally Holding Property

There is no tax advantage or disadvantage to holding property simply in your name. However, there is tremendous risk in holding property without the benefit of a limited liability business structure.

Partnership

Partnership tax law is very favorable for real estate holdings. One benefit of partnership tax law is the tremendous flexibility. Distributions from a partnership come out at basis, not the fair market value of the S corporation distributions. This allows you to move assets in and out without tax consequence. The partnership is also a very easy structure in which to do a Section 1031 like-kind tax-deferred exchange.

Partnership income, including both passive rents and capital gains income, flows through to the individual owners and the tax is paid at their level.

There are two types of partnerships—the general and the limited partnership. The general partnership is a bad entity and is never recommended. The limited partnership, however, is a tried and true entity used for real estate holdings. In some states, the limited partnership is the preferred entity for real estate holdings. In most states, however, the limited liability company (LLC), when taxed as a partnership, is the preferred structure.

Limited Liability Company (LLC)

When it comes to taxes, an LLC is a unique creature. The LLC can elect how it wants to be taxed. In the case of real estate holdings, we want the LLC to be taxed as a partnership (if there is more than one member) or under regular Schedule E tax rules if there is only one member.

If the partnership taxation is elected, a Form 1065 (U.S. partnership return) must be filed. If a single-member LLC is involved, the information will be reported on the Schedule E of the Form 1040, just as it would be if there were no LLC involved. Don't worry—you still have the asset protection!

Joint Ownership—Possible 1031 Exchange

If you plan on having multiple owners in a property and the property may be a candidate for a future like-kind exchange, it is best to hold the property as tenants in common. If you hold your property as tenants in common, you can still protect your interest with a single-member LLC. In other words, if you buy property with Fred, you and Fred will title the property as tenants in common, with the individual owners on the title being your individually owned LLC and Fred's individually owned LLC. In this way, you are in compliance with the new rules regarding multiple owners and future Section 1031 exchanges and still get the asset protection you need.

Other Real Estate Activities

As we have discussed previously in the book, real estate is a product, not a plan. There are many different things you can do with it. The recommendation we make for an LLC or LP to hold the property assumes that you are engaged in real estate investing.

Other activities such as real estate sales (as an agent or broker), construction, contracting, or quick flips are actually business activities. Unfortunately, when it comes to business activities, there is no one quick answer to the question of what is the best entity.

In *Loopholes of the Rich: How the Rich Legally Make More Money and Pay Less Tax,* there are four chapters devoted to the issue of determining the best structure for your business. Here is a summary of the factors to consider:

1. *Income:* What is your current and projected income from your business? What type of income (earned, passive, portfolio) will you create? How much and what type of other income do you receive now and how much do you predict for the future?

2. *Opportunities:* What are the opportunities for this business? Don't consider just the income—think about potential intellectual property, franchising, international opportunities, and so forth. The best short-term plan now will also plan for the future.

3. *Funding:* What kind of funding requirements will you have? How will you raise that money?

4. *Exit Strategy:* What is your exit strategy for the business? Do you intend to sell the business, pass it on to your family, or close it down? If you sell it, what would your buyer purchase—assets or stock?

5. *Appreciating Assets:* As discussed in this book, real estate is an appreciating asset and as such you want to hold it within something with partnership law.

6. *Risk:* What type of risk do you have from this business? What is your risk tolerance?

LLC for Real Estate Investing

There are three reasons why the LLC (or LP) is the best structure for tax purposes for real estate investing. These are:

1. Capital gains treatment,
2. Tax benefit for flow-through passive losses; and
3. Potential distribution of assets.

More on these items follows.

CAPITAL GAINS

The LLC or LP is a flow-through entity with the gains and losses flowing through to the individual taxpayer. If you sell the property at a future time, the gain from the sale is subject to capital gains. In this case, you will want to have individual tax rates applied, as the capital gains treatment for an individual is less than that for a corporation.

TAX BENEFIT

The LLC or LP might also flow through passive losses, particularly if Loophole #2, "Accelerating Depreciation," and Loophole #3, "Real Estate Professional," have been used. You want those benefits for yourself! Make sure you use the flow-through type entity.

DISTRIBUTIONS

So far, an S corporation could also provide the flow-through of capital gains and tax benefits. One potential problem occurs if you ever decide to distribute out all or some of the property. The key here is flexibility. You lose that option with an S corporation. For example, let's assume that you have a large piece of property and then, later, are able to subdivide the property into more than one piece. Sometimes you don't even plan it! In one case, an acre of a large piece of property was taken by the state (after they paid a nice price for it!). This now created two pieces of property. In some cases, you may not want to have the properties held in the same entity. But you'd be stuck if you're in an S corporation.

You can distribute property from an LLC or LP at basis. There would be no taxable event. It simply moves out at whatever value it is held on the books at.

On the other hand, if the property was held in an S corporation, the property must distribute out at the current fair market value. That means there is likely to be a taxable event as the property hopefully has appreciated as you have held it. To distribute means to pay tax. But if you wait to distribute, the situation will only worsen.

99 Percent of the Time

As we've repeated throughout this book, there is no one answer that is always right for all circumstances when it comes to legal and tax planning. However, there is one answer that is *almost always* right in determining the best entity to use to hold your property for tax purposes. For the reasons stated above, we generally recommend that clients hold their properties in an LLC or LP.

Part Four

Introduction to Selection Secrets

We have just learned how to benefit from the powerful tax and legal loopholes used by successful real estate investors. Knowing and using these key strategies will provide you with a distinct advantage in all of your real estate activities.

Now that you know and appreciate the loopholes associated with real estate investing, it is time to use this information to select the right property.

By selection secrets we are not referring to the constant chatter as to location du jour. Whether Phoenix is the hot market this year or Atlanta looks good next year, whether Reno is up and coming and Spokane is still five years off, is not the issue.

It is crucial to know that there are real estate opportunities at any time in any market. Do not give up improving your life through real estate holdings simply because you are not near what someone else has anointed as a hot or soon to be hot real estate market. The opportunities are everywhere, and are as close as you need them to be.

By engaging in a thoughtful property analysis and conducting the necessary due diligence and investigative review, you will be able to find real estate to your liking in the location of your liking.

So let's review and understand the secrets for selecting the right property for you.

Chapter 22

Property Analysis

What Is Your Plan?

Before you do the number crunching of property analysis, you need to know what you want. Are you planning to invest for cash flow or invest for appreciation? Or are you planning on investing based on a hybrid of both? If your plan is to develop property, that's yet another whole different plan.

Property Development

If your investment strategy is to develop property, you will need to do a thorough analysis of the budgets. If you have never been a property developer before, make sure you have experienced and successful developers and their advisors on your team. Each individual property, and its legal constraints and considerations, will be different. Closely perform market analysis both of the current property, in its current state, and the value of the developed property. Don't buy a property based on the value it could be. Buy the property at its current value, in its current state.

Too many people jump into the property development business, lured by the promise of huge returns, without understanding all of the work necessary to make it happen. Property development makes more millionaires . . . and leads to more bankruptcies . . . than any other form of real estate investment.

Investing for Cash Flow

If you have determined to invest for cash flow, make that your primary focus. Don't let yourself get swayed into becoming a real estate speculator or into making quick flips unless the property simply doesn't lend itself to cash flow.

Cash flow investing is a slow plan. You won't get rich quick, but you will surely get rich with little money and time.

There are five steps to getting started with cash flow investing:

1. Identify the type of property. Do you want to invest using something like the Rent to Buy program? Are you instead looking for multi-family units? Assess your assets first. How much money do you have to invest? How much of a loan can you qualify for?

2. Identify the area to invest in. We recommend that your first few investments be in your own area. It will be easier to work with a real estate agent (at least initially) and you will be more familiar with trends in your own area. Typically, working-class neighborhoods will provide the best return on cash. Higher-end properties require more money down, which means you have more cash invested. In order to have a good cash-on-cash return, you need to clear (income in excess of costs) more money each month. That is difficult to do on an expensive property.

3. With your team, identify suitable properties. Don't just rely on your real estate agent for this. Ask your mortgage broker, your appraiser, and your insurance agent. Ask your accountant and your attorney. Ask everyone if they know of a good deal in real estate. Just because they recommend a property, though, don't forget that it is still your responsibility to perform due diligence.

4. Assess the property. Are there cosmetic problems (not structural) that can be fixed with little effort or money? Your home inspector can help you with this. What are the comparable values of homes in the area? What are the comparable rents in the area? What is the relative value of homes in the neighborhood? Generally, you want to buy a property that is in the middle to lower part of value in the neighborhood.

5. Assess the area. After you've identified some neighborhoods to invest in, assess them. Is the area improving or declining? Every neighborhood is changing. If someone tells you it is stable, it generally is declining. Look for signs of deferred maintenance in the neighborhood. Are there a lot of "For

Sale" signs in the neighborhood? Ask your real estate agent for comparative values on properties over the past few years. Have the prices gone up or down?

WAYS TO IMPROVE CASH FLOW

Look for ways to improve your cash flow. Here are some ideas that might work:

• *Selling financing Rent to Buy:* In the Rent to Buy program, you are selling a home, financing, and, even more importantly, the hope that someone can one day own their own home.

• *Storage unit:* Apartment owners are always looking for places to store their stuff. If you have room on your property, consider building and then renting storage units on your property for your tenants.

• *Laundry:* Most apartment houses have their own laundry facility. But if you have an apartment house that doesn't—put one in! Those quarters really add up.

• *Garage, carport:* Most people want to store their cars out of the cold and heat. If your property doesn't have a garage or carport, consider putting one in if the cost is justified in increased income.

• *Updated look:* Sometimes the easiest and cheapest remodels involve updating the look of a property. Consider changing the color, wallpaper design, and flooring first. These updates aren't as expensive as structural changes, which have limited benefit relative to the cost.

• *Fence:* If other properties in the neighborhood have fences, and yours does not, consider putting a fence in.

Perceived Value Versus Engineer's Value— Diane's Comments

Richard and I used to have an ongoing debate on the changes needed for a property. He approached the property, and its construction, from his engineering background But we quickly learned that making something more solid would impress only a small percentage of the population. The bulk of the people who buy a property are looking at superficial items.

We learned that lesson with a three-bedroom, two-bathroom home in Phoenix. The first thing you noticed when you walked in was foil wallpaper and the mirror tiles. We hired two guys who spent a week removing the wallpaper and tiles and repainting the walls. At the first open house, several weeks later, curious neighbors came by. The first couple in exclaimed, "Oh, you raised the ceiling! It is so much more open now!" All we had fixed were some superficial things, but those items increased the perceived value of the home.

We updated the look and brightened the paint for a change that created a 50 percent cash-on-cash return. Not bad!

PROPERTY ANALYSIS CALCULATION

There are two very important calculations to make before you buy. Remember, you can make an offer "subject to inspection and financing," so you don't need to slow down the offer process while you do the following research. But don't neglect running these numbers before you close.

Step #1: Calculate how much cash down the property will take:

Down payment (from mortgage broker)	_____
Closing costs	_____
+ Estimated fix-up costs	_____
+ Carrying time for fix-up (number of months times monthly payment)	_____
+ Carrying time for marketing (number of months times monthly payment)	_____
= Total	_____

Now, the big question: Do you have, or can you get, that much money?

Step #2: Calculate cash-on-cash return:

Rent received	A	_____
Monthly payment, including taxes and insurance	B	_____
Cash flow (A minus B)	C	_____
Your investment (from Step #1 above)	D	_____
Amount from tenant/lessor	E	_____

The cash-on-cash % formula is:

$$(12 \times C) \div (D - E)$$

Calculate the estimated cash-on-cash return before finalizing any offer. If it's not your established minimum return, don't do the deal.

WHAT IF THE VALUE GOES DOWN?

One big advantage of investing for cash flow is that rent is king. It doesn't matter if the value of the property goes down. As long as your rent remains the same, you've still got your cash flow. You have bought the current cash flow, not the future dream of appreciation.

If your property goes down in value so dramatically that rent is affected, it will only be a temporary problem. In other words, if you could only rent the property for half its normal rent, you would have a negative cash flow only until the time when the rents went up.

Remember that the decision to invest should not be based on the geographic area, but rather on the specifics of the individual deal. There are deals everywhere. However, there are some geographic areas that have been heavily influenced by general economic conditions.

One of these areas is the Rust Belt of the Mid-Atlantic and Northeast United States. As people move from these areas into sunnier climates, the houses have declined in value. In fact, they have declined so dramatically that it is possible to get a duplex or two-family home for as low as $20,000 in areas of western Massachusetts and upstate New York. These properties still rent for $600 to $800 per unit. If you take the time to run that through the property analysis calculation in this chapter, you will see phenomenal returns. However, the property values in these areas are not increasing. People are still moving away from these areas and the income levels are dropping.

At the other extreme, Southern California shows huge growth potential with some areas consistently increasing 15 percent and more per year. Yet, at the same time, you can't get these properties to easily cash-flow. Rents aren't keeping up with the quickly increasing property values.

Either scenario could prove to be highly profitable—if you bought right and the property was right for your circumstance. For example, if you had very little cash reserves, it would not be a good idea to invest in an area that has good appreciation potential but little chance of cash-flowing, no matter how good the deal was. But if you bought a personal residence with minimal down, held it for two years, 15 percent per year appreciation could equate to more than 600 percent cash-on-cash return . . . tax-free! All you have to do is move.

Investing for Appreciation

The two rules to remember when investing for appreciation are actually warnings:

    1. How long could you afford to hold the property if you lost your current job? In other words, investing for appreciation typically means a small or negative cash flow. How many of these deals can you really afford?

    2. What is your return if you can't sell the house as quickly as you thought? If you expect to double your money, but it takes you ten years to make a sale, the return would be much lower than on a cash-flowing property.

This is probably the single biggest mistake first-time investors make. They get lured by the prospect of doubling (or more) their money, but fail to take into account the amount of money it will take to stay in the game and the time it may take to sell the property. Investing for appreciation can work—but only if the circumstances are right both for you and for the property.

The one time that investing for appreciation is a smart tax move is with your principal residence. More on how to take advantage of the principal residence tax-free strategy is in Chapter 8, "Loophole #1: Principal Residence."

SAFETY CUSHION

You've probably seen the programs on television that advertise how you can get out of debt. But you've also read in this book about the power of leverage. How can you get both the comfort of knowing you won't lose your property in a downturn with the power of leverage?

We recommend that you set aside a safety cushion.

Safety Cushion—Diane's Comments

Richard and I have put aside three months' worth of mortgage payments on all properties. This assumes that if there is no income from our businesses to cover expenses PLUS all the tenants move out at once, we can still afford the property payments for three months. Those are pretty dire circumstances, but we are still covered . . . at least for three months.

I was asked last year by one of our DKA clients my opinion on his refinancing his home. He had an investment property that he wanted to purchase and the refinance could provide the funds for buying the property. He and his wife were worried about the increased payment that would result from the refinanced amount of $50,000 coming from their personal residence. The concern was the $400 payment increase due to the $50,000 "withdrawal." They had an option of investing the $50,000 into a property that would give them a return of $1,000 per month (and cost them an additional $400) or doing nothing. We determined that they felt they could turn any bad circumstance around in six months, so a six-month cushion was established. They made the investment and everyone was happy. Ironically, they sold the home for a profit six months later and moved into another home. The concern turned out to be unfounded.

Of course, everyone's plan is different. Some people view debt in any circumstance as risky and no matter how large the cushion is, they won't be comfortable. It's all a matter of choice.

ANALYSIS OF A PROPERTY HELD FOR APPRECIATION

The best indicator of future appreciation will be the past appreciation, and recessionary, cycles. Your real estate broker should be able to help you with the past valuation trends in your area. Take a long-term view of the cycles. Does the property appear to be growing with every cycle? Can you see a pattern for the appreciation? For example, some areas of Southern California more or less have a seven-year cycle. If there is an identifiable cycle, can you project where the property is in the current cycle?

One strong indicator is whether it is a buyers' market (more sellers than buyers) or a sellers' market (more buyers than sellers). In a buyers' market, you want to buy because you have more people trying to sell than people trying to buy. This is an instance of when you can make a good deal on the price. The risk is that the market will continue to decline and you might have bought too early.

In a sellers' market, there is a lot of competition for the homes being sold. The deals tend to be properties that are a little different. When there is an active real estate market, the agents will concentrate on the quick and easy sales. They don't have time for property that isn't tiptop or that needs remodeling. You can make better deals on these properties during these times. Of course, the sellers can be more difficult to negotiate with as you won't have the agent adding objectivity.

Chapter 23

Legal Due Diligence

Once you have analyzed the property from an income suitability perspective you need to move to the next selection criteria. Acquiring investment property must involve a certain measure of legal due diligence, or investigation. You want to make sure that the property you are buying is free from claims and problems, which can range from environmental and hazardous waste issues to structural and electrical concerns.

Preparing the Offer

How do you protect yourself and get the time to complete your due diligence review?

By preparing the offer to purchase in such a way that your investigation is a contingency for purchase. If you don't like what your investigation reveals, the contingency language in the offer can give you the right to back out of the deal, no questions asked, with all deposits refunded. For example, an offer may read something like this:

> This offer is contingent upon buyer's inspection of the property and acceptance of its condition within 30 days from acceptance.

In some states, the inspection period may be in the ten to fifteen-day range. As well, some sellers may request a shorter time period in order to move things along. Nevertheless, assuming a thirty-day period, if the offer is accepted by the seller on March 1, you have until March 31 to inspect the property and accept the shape it is in or, as an alternative, request the necessary repairs be made. If March 31st comes and goes and you haven't spoken with the seller or their broker about the contingency, it will be their position that you have waived it and now accept the property's condition. The contingency is removed and the purchase may proceed.

This may not be your position. To protect yourself if you intend to get out of the deal due to the contingency, you need to send a written letter before the deadline to the seller or their broker (and preferably to both) stating that after your inspection you do not accept the property's condition and, pursuant to the express terms of the contingency, the deal is off. If you somehow miss notifying the seller during the contingency period and do not want to purchase the property, you may end up forfeiting the earnest money deposit. This, however, may be preferable to being sued for specific performance and the entire amount of the transaction.

You need to know that the good brokers, the ones who lead deals to a closing, will prepare a written statement for you to sign in which you accept the condition of the property and the contingency is removed. If this is the case and you want to buy the property, you will sign it. If it is not, obviously you won't sign the statement. Please note that in some states the contingency may be stated in the real estate contract and waived with the passage of time.

In some states sellers are required to provide a seller's property disclosure statement (SPDS), which is intended to identify material facts about the property. Nevertheless, an SPDS should not be considered an alternative to your own due diligence. For example, on the front of Arizona's SPDS the following warning is provided:

Message to the Buyer

The information contained in the SPDS is a disclosure of the Seller's actual knowledge of the Property and not a representation of every possible defect. It is not a warranty of any kind. You should confirm any information you consider material to your purchase and consider obtaining a professional property inspection, which may reveal information about the Property that even the seller did not know.

> THE FOLLOWING ARE REPRESENTATIONS MADE BY THE SELLER AND
> ARE NOT THE REPRESENTATIONS OF THE AGENT(S), IF ANY. THIS IN-
> FORMATION IS A DISCLOSURE AND IS NOT INTENDED TO BE PART
> OF ANY CONTRACT BETWEEN THE BUYER AND SELLER.

As a result, you will want your contract to provide due diligence flexibility. There are a number of contingencies that can be used to both give you time to investigate and let you out if you don't like what you find. These include:

- Review for hazardous waste conditions
- Obtaining acceptable financing
- Acceptance of all leases and contracts
- Acceptance of the title report and all documents referenced in the title report

The contingency for acceptable financing is an excellent out to use in an offer. Who can objectively say what is or is not acceptable financing? You may be able to obtain a 6 percent fixed and fully amortized thirty-year loan and, in your sole and absolute discretion, decide this is unacceptable and get out of the deal. Buyers should always consider using the acceptable financing contingency.

Two major property issues arise for which due diligence is imperative. You will want to be sure that your offer includes contingencies for a title report and a hazardous waste review. We shall explore both issues.

Understanding Preliminary Title Reports

After spending countless hours analyzing and considering the right investment property with your real estate agent, viewing property after property, having the proper inspections performed, and considering various forms of financing, you think you have found the perfect investment. But is it? Although the property seems flawless, there may be lingering issues that you need to face. Undoubtedly, you have thought about the purchase price, the neighborhood, and the physical properties of the structure. However, more than these obvious factors affect an interest in real estate.

When you purchase investment property, you purchase more than a house or other structure. You purchase an interest in real estate and all the problems that may follow. Your ability to use the property as you please or to sell the property may be affected by flaws in the title to the property. These flaws include easements (whereby someone else has a right to use your property for a certain purpose), restrictions (whereby your use of the property may be limited), or other property interests held by third parties. If the flaws are not to your liking, using your title report contingency, you will not purchase the property.

However, sometimes the flaws are subtle. One way of protecting against them is to acquire title insurance. As a practical matter, lenders will not advance monies until a clear title report has been received and title insurance is in place.

Title insurance companies generally insure against defects in, or liens or encumbrances on, the title to a piece of property. If a title dispute arises in the future and it involves a risk covered by your title insurance, the title insurance company probably will not compensate you for your losses. However, title insurance companies will aid in defending against challenges to your title to the property. Because title insurance companies will only assist you in those matters that they agreed to insure against, it is important to know the extent of your coverage.

Why Is a Preliminary Title Report Important?

Before a title insurance company will issue insurance on the title to the property and accordingly before you can obtain funding from your lender, the title insurance company will issue a preliminary title report. The preliminary title report is the product of the title insurance company's review of public records related to the property you hope to purchase. A preliminary title report is not a guarantee and cannot be relied upon in most states as a representation of the status of title to the property. The preliminary title report provides you with the limits and extents to which the title insurance company is willing to insure the title to the property.

The final insurance policy should include all the terms and limitations presented in the preliminary title report. The exceptions listed on the preliminary title report and the final insurance contract are the risks the title insurance company has refused to insure against. Should a problem arise at some later date, the title insurance company will become involved only if it is one of the problems the insurer agreed to insure against.

When you receive the preliminary title report from your title insurance company, it is essential that you review and understand the report. Although many real estate transactions include title insurance and preliminary title reports, this is not always enough. Far too often, the seller and/or buyer fail to read or understand the preliminary title report. As a result, no questions are raised. Only after the real estate transaction is closed does the buyer discover that they may not have title insurance for problems that existed and were disclosed in the preliminary title report. At that point, you cannot change the terms of the purchase agreement to protect yourself against risks that the title insurance company refuses to insure against.

To protect your interests and ensure that the real estate you think you want is actually right for you, you need to take the time to carefully review the preliminary title report or have your lawyer review it for you. By reviewing the preliminary title report, you may ensure that you have sufficient title insurance coverage. Additionally, you may then negotiate the terms of the real estate purchase agreement to protect yourself against risks that cannot be insured against.

What Should I Look for in My Preliminary Title Report?

The first thing to look for is any inaccuracies or inconsistencies between your understanding of the target property and the description of the property provided on the preliminary title report. If you find any, you need to discuss the issue with your attorney and title insurance company. While some issues may require you to seek additional assurances from the seller or work with the seller to resolve any problems with title to the property, you should make sure that you understand the importance of the information provided on the preliminary title report before you confront the seller. Nevertheless, by reviewing the preliminary title report yourself you are ensuring that you are making an informed decision and playing an active role in your real estate purchase.

Most preliminary title reports include the following elements, which should each be reviewed for accuracy:

• *Addressee:* Generally, the party who will close the transaction, prepare the contract, or close the loan. Copies of the report are sent to the seller, buyer/borrower real estate agent, lender, and attorney if requested. You should make sure that all names and addresses are correct.

• *Current Owner (Vested Owner):* This is generally the name of the seller of the property. As with everything else, you should make sure that this is accurate.

• *Legal Description of the Property:* This should be the same as the legal description provided in the real estate purchase agreement. You should carefully compare the descriptions to make sure that the title insurance policy will cover all of the property you hope to purchase. If the description on the preliminary title report differs from that provided in the real estate purchase agreement, the title company may not have performed a title search on the excluded property and may not be willing to insure title to the excluded property.

• *Plat Map:* If included, this will describe the lot size and may identify street names and the nearest intersection. A significant amount of residential property was once a subdivision of land. Plat maps represent the division and show streets created with the subdivision. This may give rise to easements affecting your land. Some property is sold with reference to a plat map. You should make sure that there is no discrepancy between the plat map and the legal description of the property.

• *Type of Estate or Interest:* This is the type of interest in property you will acquire from the seller. Property interests differ, and it is important that you understand the type of property interest that you will acquire from the seller. The most common and broadest form of property interest is the fee simple absolute. If any other form of property interest is indicated on the preliminary title report or in the purchase agreement, you should make sure that you understand the limitations on the interest you are acquiring. A discussion of land ownership is found in Chapter 16.

• *Effective Date:* This is the limit on the scope of the preliminary title report. Title insurance companies generally have a collection of public records, known as a title plant, which they use in preparing title reports. The effective date indicates the date through which the title plant is current. The title report covers facts known through that date.

• *Type of Policy Requested:* This should include the limit of liability the insurance company will assume, the premium to be paid, and other details regarding your relationship with the insurance company. You should make sure that the policy indicated in the preliminary title report is the same policy you discussed with the title insurance agent.

• *Report Number and Contact Person:* The report number and contact person will become necessary if you have any questions regarding the report. You should use the report number to direct questions to the agent handling your file.

In addition to the foregoing, a preliminary title report will contain valuable information about the limitations on the insurance policy the insurer is willing to offer you. These limitations are expressed as the exceptions to the title insurance policy. In addition, the exceptions provide you with information about the limitations or restrictions on the property you want to purchase. Common exceptions and a description of their implications are provided below:

• *Easements:* As indicated above, easements are rights to use your land that other people or the general public may possess. Exclusions based on easements may or may not adversely affect the property you hope to purchase. Nevertheless, it is important for you to notice and consider the impact of existing easements. Easements may include the following:

1. A right of way: a third party's right to use a path or road across your property;

2. A utility easement or right to place or keep something on the land: a third party's right to use and maintain a sewer pipe, telephone line, garage, or any other thing on your property or across your property;

3. A right of entry: Allows a third party to enter your property for certain defined purposes;

4. A right to the support of land and buildings: Applicable, for example, if you are purchasing a lower-story apartment in an apartment complex;

5. A right of light and air: Provides a third party a right that may limit your ability to build or otherwise use your property if your use interferes with their rights;

6. A right to water: Provides a third party a right to use a waterway or divert water from a waterway located on or adjacent to your property; and

7. A right to do some act that would otherwise amount to a nuisance.

• *Covenants, Conditions, and Restrictions:* Also referred to as CC&Rs, these may limit your ability to use or sell the property and are enforceable by the seller or third parties. While a breach of covenants or restrictions may result in financial liability, some forms of conditions may cause ownership of the property to revert to a prior owner or some third party. CC&Rs may include things such as a prohibition on brightly colored exterior paint, limitations on use of the property for business purposes, building limitations, and the like. Again, these may or may not adversely affect the property you hope to purchase, but you should notice and consider the impact CC&Rs make on the property, your ability to use the property as you want, and your ability to sell the property.

• *Mortgage or Deed of Trust:* These arise from loans taken against the property. Depending upon the system used in your state, an existing mortgage or deed of trust may directly affect title to the property or may create a potential for a lien or foreclosure and sale of the property. Accordingly, it is important to determine whether the seller may actually convey the property subject to the mortgage or deed of trust and whether the mortgage or deed of trust will affect the nature of the property interest you may purchase.

• *Notice of Default:* This exception indicates that there is an existing foreclosure proceeding against the property. If the property is subject to an existing foreclosure proceeding, you will not want to independently purchase it, but may want to purchase it as part of the foreclosure proceeding. Be sure to check with a local attorney before venturing into foreclosure purchases.

• *Parties in Possession:* This exception indicates that rights or claims of parties currently possessing the property that are not recorded in the public records are excluded from the coverage. This may include the rights of someone who is wrongfully in possession of the property. To protect against such interests of parties in possession, you should have the property surveyed and make sure that no third party is in possession of any part of the property you hope to purchase.

• *Survey Exception:* This exception indicates rights or claims of parties in possession and easements or claims of easement not shown by the public records, boundary line disputes, overlaps, encroachments, and any matters not of record that would be disclosed by an accurate survey and inspection of the land. As in a parties in possession exception, you may protect against this exception or possibly have the exception removed by having a survey and inspection of the property performed.

- *Mechanics' Liens:* This exception indicates that any lien, or right to a lien, for services, labor, or material furnished for prior or subsequent development of the property will be excluded from the insurance policy. This exception is problematic, in that mechanics' liens may not appear on record even though they exist, because a mechanics' lien often takes effect when the work begins, but is not recorded until after the work is completed and the current owner fails to pay for the work. To ensure protection against mechanics' liens, you may seek to have the seller warranty against mechanics' liens. Some title companies will work with buyers and sellers who have the proper documents in place and will cover on mechanics' liens.

- *State or Federal Tax Liens, Judgments, Bankruptcy:* This exception limits the title insurance coverage to exclude taxes, assessments, and judicial proceedings that are not shown as existing liens by the public records. A warranty from the seller that no such proceedings or limitations on the property exist may provide you with a remedy if such threats to the property arise. Notice of default is important. If bankruptcy is an issue, most title companies will hold insurance until a court order removing the property from the bankruptcy court's jurisdiction has been filed.

While the foregoing are common provisions that you may find in your preliminary title report, other provisions may affect the property interest you acquire. When you receive your preliminary title report, you should carefully review all the information it contains to ensure that it represents your understanding of the property you hope to purchase. After all the work you have done to find the perfect piece of real estate, the task of reading through a preliminary title report and acquiring title insurance is not overly burdensome. However, it is one of the many steps necessary to protect yourself against risks and ensure that your hard work in finding the property was not time wasted. By devoting the necessary time and energy to your investment, you will avoid regret and guarantee success.

Understanding Environmental Concerns

Another very important due diligence item is the review and understanding of environmental issues affecting the property. You will want to include a contingency in the offer covering the review and acceptance of the property's environmental condition.

The importance of this issue is illustrated in the following case.

Karen, LaVerne, and Hooper

Karen and LaVerne were new to real estate investing. Karen had been fortunate enough to receive a large cash settlement from her Uncle Arnold's estate and was looking for a good property to invest in. LaVerne was Karen's best friend, and while she didn't have as much money to invest as did Karen, LaVerne was a good handyperson, and so Karen had agreed that they would own the property 50–50, with LaVerne's handiwork around the property being valued to make up the difference in money being invested.

The two friends were looking at a downtown area that was undergoing a renaissance. It was full of friendly, sunny, pedestrian-oriented streets lined with small shops and grocery stands. Karen and LaVerne soon found a property that they liked, a newer four-plex built right on the corner of a quiet street.

The property had been owned by Mr. Hooper, who told the pair that he had owned the land for many years. He had torn down the previous structure and put up the four-plex about five years ago, to cash in on the redevelopment opportunities. He had made a tidy pile off the four-plex in the five-year period and was leaving the area to live out his retirement years closer to his son.

Karen and LaVerne liked the property because with a newer four-plex, they reasoned, it could be rented out for higher rents than some of the surrounding older buildings, and it wouldn't need as much maintenance. They also liked the fact that Mr. Hooper had owned the land for so many years, as that gave them a good history into the land use. They went back to talk to Mr. Hooper about making an offer and having the property inspected thoroughly before closing the deal.

Mr. Hooper was in a hurry to leave town and join his son, so he made the pair a deal. He would knock $10,000 off the asking price if they would agree to sign the paperwork and close the deal within twenty-one days. Karen and LaVerne were pleased with their good fortune, and signed on the dotted line. Although the quick deadline did not give them enough time to have the property inspected as thoroughly as they wanted, they did have time to have a structural inspection done, which revealed no defects in the four-plex's construction. Besides, if Mr. Hooper had owned the land for so many years, they felt sure he would have mentioned any problems in the land's history.

The deal was closed, the four-plex changed hands, and Karen and LaVerne entered the world of property ownership and management. The existing tenants remained, the rents were paid on time, and life was good.

Until one of the tenants began complaining of problems in his portion of the garden. The plants had begun to die off, and no matter how many times they were replaced, the results were the same. LaVerne looked over the garden and told the tenant that perhaps there were some bugs or blight in the soil, and the tenant should consider replacing it.

A few weeks later, Karen got a call from the same tenant, complaining that now the grass had suddenly died off in his portion of the four-plex's garden, and in the neighboring portion as well. Karen and LaVerne went to view the garden and found the lawn completely withered. LaVerne did not know what the problem was, so Karen decided to call in a soil expert, to see what had caused the plant life to die off.

The news was not good. Unbeknownst to Karen and LaVerne, before the four-plex had been built, Mr. Hooper had run a gas station on the land for over twenty years. When the gas station was torn down to make way for the four-plex, Mr. Hooper hadn't bothered to have the underground gas storage tanks removed. The tanks were now over twenty-five years old and were beginning to disintegrate. Old fuel had been leaking into the ground around the tanks for the past several years, and was now reaching the surface.

Karen and LaVerne were in trouble. The tanks had to be removed immediately, to stop any further environmental contamination. If they didn't they would face lawsuits from the tenants for allowing a dangerous condition to exist on the property. They also faced the risk that a plume of contaminated oil would affect other neighboring properties, thus increasing their liability. And it was quite likely that the environmental authorities would demand an immediate and expensive environmental remediation. The only remedy was to remove the tanks, which meant first tearing down the four-plex.

LaVerne was furious. She spoke with Mr. Davies, her attorney, and asked what could be done about the situation. There was some insurance over the property, but not enough to cover having it torn down, the tanks removed, the tenants relocated, and the property reconstructed. LaVerne thought that Mr. Hooper should be held accountable—surely he had a duty to tell the pair the truth about the property's history? Mr. Davies agreed that Karen and LaVerne had a good case against the former property owner for misrepresentation, and that they might be able to recover a large portion of the monies the pair were now looking at spending to remediate their four-plex. Mr. Davies drew up the court papers and filed them, and sent a process server to track down Mr. Hooper.

Unfortunately, although the process server was able to locate Mr. Hooper's son in Iowa, he found that Mr. Hooper had died about six months ago. His meager estate had been settled and distributed. And, upon his death, the ability of Karen and LaVerne to collect from him some of the costs they were going to incur in the remediation of the four-plex was lost.

There was nothing else that Karen and LaVerne could do. They had enough money from the insurance policy to relocate the tenants, tear down the four-plex, and remove the leaking fuel tanks. However, they did not have enough money to complete the reclamation project and rebuild the four-plex, and were forced to sell the property at a bargain-basement price and walk away. Both considered themselves fortunate to not have been fined, jailed, or forced into bankruptcy. When last seen, Karen and LaVerne were sharing a small apartment to save expenses, and argued constantly.

The consequence of hazardous waste and other environmental maladies on your property are devastating. Federal and state authorities will hold you responsible for the cleanup whether you made the mess or not. And know that environmental remediation is extremely expensive.

How Can You Protect Yourself?

First, you need to appreciate who is a responsible party.

Federal law basically holds four classes of parties responsible for cleanup of a hazardous waste site:

1. The current owner and operator of the property.
2. The owner and operator of the property at the time the waste was deposited.
3. Those who generated the waste and sent it to the site.
4. Those who transported waste to the site.

If you are the current owner, and the pollution occurred fifty years and five owners prior to your ownership, you are still a responsible party.

It is also important to appreciate that a responsible party is strictly liable.

This means that all the government has to prove in court is that there is waste on the site. It is an easy case to make, since any excuse or defense you may offer is of no use. With waste on the property you are liable, strictly and without exception.

Given the draconian nature of the system, you will not want to purchase any property that has any sort of environmental concern associated with it. Leave those problem properties for remediation experts or, if no one else can be held responsible for it, the government to fix.

But what about a property where you don't know if there's a problem or not? If you buy it and a problem turns up, you are responsible and liable. How do you protect yourself?

By having state-licensed engineers prepare a Phase I environmental report, which is a survey of potential environmental problems on the property. The engineers do an inspection and if no problems appear they will say so in a written report. If a concern shows up, they may suggest preparation of a Phase II environmental report, which is more detailed. However, if you can't get a clean Phase I on the property you most likely aren't going to want to buy it. And even if you are, the bank isn't going to loan on it.

If you get a clean Phase I report, thus satisfying your environmental contingency, and you go ahead and buy the property, be sure to save the report. A clean Phase I report will protect you into the future. Within the federal law there is the "innocent landowner defense." It requires a landowner to prove that at the time of purchase they "did not know and had no reason to know that any hazardous substance . . . was disposed of on, in, or at the facility" [42 U.S.C. §9601 (35)(A)(i)]. If later an environmental issue should arise, the fact that you intended to comply with the environmental laws by having an engineer check out the property before your purchase and the property was reported as clear, is a handy argument to have.

In Appendix B we have included a checklist of environmental documents you may want to review prior to purchasing a property.

Another hazardous waste issue can arise from within your building. If you have a tenant operating a methamphetamine lab in one of your apartments you will be responsible for a toxic cleanup. A room housing a meth lab will have to be torn down to the timbers and expensively remediated by specially qualified personnel. It is prudent to know who your tenants are and what they are doing.

Due Diligence Checklists

In the selection process it is useful to review checklists of items that may or may not be issues in your property purchase. By using a checklist you can remind yourself of an issue you had forgotten or failed to follow through on. You can take it upon yourself to handle a matter your broker is unwilling or too busy to tackle.

The checklists we have included in Appendix B are by no means comprehensive and are not intended to serve as the absolute and correct model to the exclusion of other questions and issues. Nevertheless, they do serve to raise issues you should be concerned with in your due diligence review. The more investigation you conduct to your satisfaction the more comfortable you will be that you are selecting the right property.

Chapter 24

Real-Life Selection Stories

As we set out at the beginning of this book, both of the authors are working to build wealth through real estate investments. One of the things that we have done in researching this book is talk to many people involved in various aspects of real estate investment to gain information and insights into the challenges around differing types of properties. In this chapter, we will present some real-life selection stories.

Selecting Properties, Selecting Managers (Garrett's Story)

My career in investment real estate began by accident. Although licensed as a California real estate broker for many years, I had never actually owned real estate until I purchased my first starter house in a quaint and pleasant Reno neighborhood. Later, after marrying Jenny and having Ted, it was time to move to a bigger place. But when we considered selling the house it became clear that we would lose money on it. After broker's fees, transfer fees, and all the rest, it was cheaper to keep it and rent it out. And for me, cheaper is almost always better.

I soon learned the not very complex issues involved with leasing property you own to those who don't own it and could care less about it—until, of course, something breaks. The main issue involved a tenant who always had an excuse for untimely payment of rent. For me it was a culture shock. Whenever I had rented a place I had never turned in a late rent payment. Whether it was fear or guilt or parents who just thoroughly drilled in me the importance of timeliness, I had never once paid a late fee. And then, all of a sudden, as a landlord for a tenant to be so casual and unconcerned about meeting their obligation was both frustrating and amazing. While having been in the trenches as a lawyer and dealing with other people's problems and lack of follow-through on contracts, it was still a very personal and annoying affront to have a tenant not pay on time on *my* property. I had a mortgage to pay and the tenant's excuses weren't legal tender.

I was also too busy to deal with it all. My time was better spent doing what I do to earn money and letting a professional real estate management firm do what they do to manage the property and earn a fee. I interviewed several management companies and came up with one that had a good local business reputation and understanding of the market, as well as a fee structure that was fair and reasonable. For 10 percent of the gross rental revenues on the little house, the company paid all the bills, inspected and arranged for repairs, and lined up any new non–excuse-filled tenants as needed. By my calculations of the value of my time, it was costing me twice that amount to take care of the property myself.

I have been satisfied ever since, especially since my only contact with the company is a monthly statement.

Then of course, I forgot my lesson. Several years later things had improved and it was time to buy a bigger property, in this case a larger apartment building. For 10 percent of the gross rents I could certainly manage it myself.

So Barb the bookkeeper and I set about lining up vendors and handling repairs, paying bills and collecting rents, handling the bookkeeping, setting up new leases, and doing everything else involved with managing such a property.

And whereas with the little house I only had one tenant offering up excuses, now I had a chorus of them, a cacophony of weird, wonderful, and just plain lame excuses such as:

"I am an artist. I don't pay rent."

"I misplaced my rent money in a bar."

"There was an earthquake. So I can't pay." "Oh, I see . . . umm, where was the earthquake?" "Back east."

"The Raiders lost again."

"My rent was detained at the border."

"The Federal Reserve has left us without a real currency."

"My wife met my girlfriend."

Again, for someone who lives with a fairly strict view of timeliness and fulfillment of obligations, it was as if these casual, half-baked excuses were delivered by aliens. From a more grounded viewpoint, it occurred to me that I was managing not an apartment building but a nursery school.

The crowning blow came when a tenant called my law office, insisted that I be pulled out of a meeting, and, when I got on the phone, demanded that I come down to the building immediately. When I asked what the problem was, she informed me that someone had left their laundry in the dryer. She needed it removed so she could use the dryer, but didn't know whether the laundry was sanitary, so would not touch the offending laundry. She wanted me to come down and do it.

I started interviewing management companies that afternoon.

Selecting and Using Property Management Companies

My initial concern that the companies would all charge a fee based on 10 percent of the gross rentals was unfounded. Some were half that but with various extra and reasonable charges included. Nevertheless, once again, based on the value of one's time, it made all the sense in the world to have a management company handle the property.

For some, managing your own property will be a cost-saving and even enjoyable task. There are some who like the tenant interaction, repair tinkering, and sense of accomplishment that such an activity provides.

For others, myself included, the job of managing is better left to others. And so, when it comes to selecting a property for investment purposes, a related element for some investors is selecting the right property management company.

What are some of the key elements to consider in selecting a management company? The following are important:

- *Local Reputation and References:* You want a company that has a reputation for integrity and honesty. Remember, they are handling your money.
- *Market Knowledge:* The company will be setting rents to maximize your investment. You want them to be experts on what the market will bear.
- *Vendor and Service Contracts:* A good management company will have strong relations with vendor and service providers. These relationships should result in lower costs for maintenance and upkeep than you may be able to obtain individually.

Once you have narrowed your search to several firms you will want to carefully review their management contracts. Items to consider include:

- *Compensation for Services:* Management companies are usually paid on a percentage of gross rental receipts, which can range from 5 percent to 10 percent. Remember, a percentage gives them an incentive to keep the property fully rented.
- *Management Duties and Responsibilities:* The contract should clearly spell out who is responsible for what. Personally, as an owner, I want some oversight but not an active, daily role.
- *The Term and Termination Clauses:* If the company is not doing the job you want to be able to give thirty days' notice and move on to the next company.
- *Spending Issues:* It needs to be set out how much can be spent without the owner's consent. Obviously, larger repairs and improvements should be presented to the owner for approval.
- *Special Contract Issues:* Be sure to read every paragraph. In some contracts you may find that the management company wants a percentage of the brokerage commission if you sell the building. These and other such nonstandard provisions should be avoided or removed.

- *Reports:* As an owner, you will want to receive regular reports on income, expenses, and reserves. Make sure such obligations are set out in the contract.

After you sign with a management company and they get settled into the property (which may take a few months), you will want to analyze their performance. This analysis will continue on an ongoing basis. The means for measuring success may include:

- Lower vacancy rate
- Greater return to the owner
- Better collections
- Lower turnover
- Fewer complaints
- Better condition of the property

Overall, the selection of the right property management company, when combined with the right selection of investment property, can prove a winning combination for a real estate investor.

Manufacturing Profits with Mobile Homes

An expert in the area of mobile home investing is Dick, a real estate broker in Silver Springs, Nevada. Located forty-five minutes due east of Carson City, Silver Springs is on the west shore of Lake Lahontan, a large recreational lake, and is a fast-growing area attracting retirees, families, and workers for nearby distribution facilities that include UPS, Amway, and Amazon. Most of the valley in which Silver Springs sits is divided into five-acre residential lots, thus offering residents a great deal of unencumbered open space as well as unblocked vistas of surrounding high desert mountains. Here is Dick's perspective on mobile home ownership and investment opportunities:

Mobile homes are everywhere but very few real estate investors are attuned to the opportunities they offer. Certainly, with reward comes risk, and mobile homes offer certain challenges, but if done right the returns can be impressive.

First of all, mobile homes have come a long way since the days of the small, narrow trailers that many people associate with the words "mobile home." In 1976, federal laws surrounding the construction of mobile homes changed, resulting in mobile homes being renamed as "manufactured housing units." New manufactured housing units are built to very high standards, rivaling that of constructed houses, and they can look as good or better than a constructed home.

But, as the term manufactured housing implies, they provide a lower-cost alternative for millions of Americans in need of decent and affordable housing.

Regardless of the term you use, when a manufactured housing unit is properly set onto a foundation it is no longer considered either mobile or manufactured—it is now real property.

In Silver Springs, 96 percent of the housing is made up of manufactured housing units. One of the common starter investment strategies I see is for the purchase of one unit by an investor. A new three-bedroom, two-bathroom manufactured home can be purchased on the low end for $60,000. In Silver Springs, five acres of developed land with a well water and septic system as well as power and telephone lines to the property can be purchased for $35,000. With a $95,000 total price, an investor can put down 10 percent, or $9,500, and obtain a thirty-year loan for the balance. Assuming a 7 percent rate, the monthly payment is just under $575.00. The local market allows for rents of $750 to $850 per month. This same type of opportunity may be available in a number of communities across the country.

Another strategy involves purchasing used units at distressed prices and moving them to a more popular location. With some of the mines closing in central Nevada, my two partners and I purchase used units for $20,000 each. We'll then pay around $5,000 to fix them up, $7,000 to move them, and $8,000 to put the renovated units onto a secure foundation on five acres of developed land in Silver Springs costing $35,000.

With a total of $75,000 invested into the project, my partners and I will be able to turn the property around for in the neighborhood of $100,000. Typically the owners must take a note for a portion of the purchase price, and cash is needed for the purchase of the home and its repair, but the returns from such an investment strategy can be significant.

In Nevada, new legislation has just been passed allowing owners of newly manufactured housing units, or units manufactured less than five years ago and meeting certain specific criteria, to be placed anywhere in Nevada. These units may be placed into any subdivision or housing development. Among the criteria to be followed, the units must be a minimum of 1,200 square feet, properly placed onto a foundation, and converted to real property. Units placed into subdivisions or developed neighborhoods must match the quality and overall look of the other homes. The legislation also prohibits land developers from writing bylaw development codes prohibiting the placement of properly qualified manufactured housing units in the development. An attempt to bar the placement of manufactured homes into a subdivision could result in charges of discrimination being laid against the developers.

To Dick, this means that in Nevada manufactured housing units have just become even more cost-effective and real estate investment opportunities have just expanded.

Dick cautions investors as to several issues. First, in Nevada and other states, there is a specific state license for manufactured housing service and installation personnel. You should not just use any handyman to handle service and installation issues. Using an unlicensed individual may result in substandard work and increased liability exposure to you if something were to go wrong. You are better off using a bonded and licensed contractor.

Dick also warns that when purchasing a used unit a careful inspection of the underside should be made. You want to be certain that all of the water, sewer, heating ducts, electric connections, and other lines are properly installed and attached between both sides of the house. It is also important that the stands are properly set when the unit is installed so that the weight is evenly distributed. A state-licensed unit installer is usually experienced in such matters.

Other issues have to do with tenants. Dick cautions that you do not lease to those with negative credit ratings. Just as a bad tenant can ruin a single-family home, a bad tenant can completely destroy a manufactured unit. You should not be a complete absentee owner, so if you aren't nearby you will need to have a local contact or representative to keep an eye on things.

As many readers are aware, owning mobile home parks can also be a winning real estate investment. In many cases, the tenants own their unit and simply rent space from the park owner, who provides water and other utilities, security, and recreational amenities. The right park with the right, contented tenants can be very lucrative.

One manufactured housing investment strategy used successfully around the country has been to buy new land in the path of progress. The investor then puts a mobile home park on the property to generate income until the city grows out to the park, at which point the land becomes much more valuable. Frequently, although the land has appreciated, the rents at the park are also higher and the highest and best use continues to be as a mobile home park.

Many of these older parks are for sale and the path of progress parks continue to be developed. A key issue for Dick, in both cases, has to do with water. Typically, because these parks start out on the outskirts of town they have their own water system. Two issues now arise under such conditions.

The first has to do with water pressure. Fire departments are now much more strict in enforcing fire flow pressure and storage requirements. Before buying or developing you need to be cognizant of the system's capabilities.

The second water issue may be of even greater consequence. The federal government is implementing new arsenic reduction standards for water systems, beginning in 2006. Although two extensions may be filed extending this deadline until 2012, the day will arrive when costly arsenic reduction requirements will have to be met. If you are buying or developing a mobile home park it is imperative to understand the nature and cost of these mandates.

Dick's final advice for would-be investors holds true for any type of real estate investment. He has seen, time and time again, out-of-area investors use out-of-area brokers, who do not know the local market. The result frequently involves the investor overpaying because their broker didn't know any better. For Dick, a cardinal rule of investing is to use area-specific real estate agents who know the local market and benefit their clients accordingly.

How Two Experienced Brokers Have Made Money in Real Estate

George and Gayle are real estate brokers in Tahoe City, California. Over the years they have represented themselves and others in the purchase of investment real estate property in California, Nevada, Arizona, and Utah. In this process George and Gayle have developed a set of guidelines for investing.

The first rule is to understand what stage of real estate investing you are in. Your goals and immediate and future needs must be analyzed. As a general rule, for the young, investing for long-term appreciation is appropriate, as is investing in fixer-uppers to be improved with sweat equity and either held or turned. For older investors, investing for cash flow should be considered. Quality properties with a solid rental history are always good, especially for later-stage investors.

George and Gayle's follow-up guidelines for investing include:

Invest in areas you know or can research easily. If you hear that Bozeman, Montana, is a hot market but can't get there frequently and have no contacts there, you may be better off staying in your local area.

You will always do better by buying in an older, established neighborhood instead of a new suburban area. The older neighborhoods will never be replicated; the suburban ones are, on a daily basis. Buy into the best neighborhood you can afford.

As a very basic rule of thumb in considering a property, check to see if the monthly rents equal 1 percent of the purchase price. For example, an investment property selling for $330,000 should generate rents of approximately $3,300 per month for a more serious inquiry to be warranted.

Talk to everyone you can about real estate. It is a popular topic of conversation and you can learn a great deal from even the most casual of discussions.

Look at every property you are considering to buy as if you were selling it. What would you do to improve it for resale? Would it be economical to fix it up for a later sale?

Look at every property you are considering from your target tenant's perspective. Is it close to public transportation and within reasonable walking distance of grocery and other shopping areas? Is the property suitable for the type of tenant you expect to rent from you? Remember that the lower the rents the bigger the pool of potential tenants.

Start investing in real estate as early as possible. It is the best pension plan ever devised.

Look into using your IRA money to invest in real estate. There are IRA administrators who will allow you to self-direct an all-cash investment into real property investments. With no debt, the monthly rents less normal expenses accumulate tax-free in your IRA account.

If a property is appreciating consider holding it instead of selling it. Then, if you can service the debt, refinance the property and use the loan proceeds to buy the next property.

Be careful when buying condominium units. If 70 percent or more of them are not owner-occupied you may be buying into a property that does not reflect pride of ownership.

If condo fees are involved, consider borrowing more money to buy a non-condo. The $100 per month paid as a condo fee is better spent on a bigger mortgage payment.

If faced with a choice between buying a two-bedroom, one-bathroom house and a three-bedroom, two-bathroom house, go with the second choice. A two-bedroom, one-bathroom house is always more difficult to sell.

Consider investing near colleges and universities. Renting to students presents certain challenges. You need to expect some damage but as long as the building is standing it can be rented. George and Gayle have had success with properties near the University of Nevada, Reno, and the University of Utah. Their clients have also generated good cash-on-cash returns at the University of Illinois—Urbana-Champaign.

Inquire as to whether the city or town has any rental control measures or other unique legislation. If so, work with a good broker to understand how such rules may be minimized or even beneficial to your program.

When selecting a real estate broker to help you, ask if they themselves own investment properties. Those who do will have a much better understanding of your needs.

George and Gayle's guidelines have come as a result of a number of successes as well as a few failures. As always, one learns much more from the deal that didn't work out.

For George and Gayle, it was a house in Long Beach, California. In the early 1970s a property was selling for $150,000 and they knew it was a good one. Great neighborhood, excellent schools, wonderful layout. But they overanalyzed the deal and got caught up in the minutiae instead of focusing on the big picture. The minor issue was $5,000 in electrical work that needed to be done. Feeling it was too much, they lost the deal to another buyer and instead bought a lesser house a mile away for $125,000.

As it turns out they doubled their money on the house they bought by selling it for $250,000. The problem was that in the same time frame, the house they passed on tripled in value, to $450,000. Their concerns over a few thousand dollars cost them a great deal more.

After that deal George and Gayle learned that their judgment and intuition were more important than overanalyzing the property. Remembering that lesson has benefited George and Gayle and can benefit you as well.

Conclusion

Congratulations. You now know the secrets that successful real estate investors have used for generations to build and protect their real estate portfolios. By using the tax, legal, and selection strategies we've discussed, you too can open and close the appropriate loopholes and successfully invest in real estate for your and your family's future.

Because the laws are constantly changing it is prudent to stay current. Both of our Web sites are updated to provide the most current information.

For updates on real estate tax laws go to www.taxloopholes.com. For current legal matters, including eviction laws and homestead exemption rules, go to www.successdna.com.

As well, because continuing education is a good thing, consider the following books and resources as worthy of your review:

> *The SuccessDNA Guide to Real Estate Investment and Management* (www.successdna.com)
>
> *Easy Accounting for Real Estate Investors* (www.successdna.com)
>
> *Loophole Strategies* (www.taxloopholes.com)
>
> *The Business Structures and Tax Loopholes Box* (www.realestate loopholes.com)
>
> *Rich Dad's Roads to Riches: 6 Steps to Becoming a Successful Real Estate Investor* (richdad.com)

How to Increase the Income from your Real Estate Investments (rich dad.com)

Real Estate Riches (Warner Books/richdad.com)

101 Ways to Massively Increase the Value of your Real Estate without Spending Much Money (www.properyprosperity.com)

With the help of your team and your broadening knowledge from readings and seminars you will succeed in real estate investing.

Good luck.

Appendix A
Frequently Asked Questions

Should my corporation hold real estate?

As a general rule, no. For tax reasons we don't recommend that you ever hold real estate in the name of a C corporation. Your C corporation will pay considerably more in capital gains when you try to sell that property than would a flow-through entity, such as an S corporation or an LLC (limited liability company). If your S corporation is holding the property and you are sued personally, a judgment creditor may be able to reach your shares in the S corporation and effectively take control of those shares and, through them, control of the S corporation and its assets. For these reasons we recommend that real estate be held in either an LLC or a limited partnership (LP). As well, transferring property out of an S corporation is a taxable event whereas it is not taxable in an LLC or an LP.

Even if it doesn't own it, can I use my corporation to buy real estate?

Yes. One method is to have your corporation pay rent for an office building that you own, held in an LLC. The rent paid by the corporation is a tax deduction for the business and the income from the rent is offset by operating expenses as well as the phantom expense of depreciation.

How else can I invest in real estate with a current corporation I have?

Since we suggest that property be held by an LLC or LP, your corporation could be a member (or partner) of that structure. In that way, the corporation can contribute money as a money partner.

What type of entity should I hold property in?

We recommend using either an LLC or an LP. Both offer flow-through income and taxation opportunities, and both offer excellent asset protection. In Nevada, for example, legislation prohibits creditors of an LLC or an LP from directly seizing assets of either type of entity. Instead, judgment creditors must secure their judgment against the LLC or limited partnership by way of the charging order procedure.

What is a charging order?

A charging order is, in essence, a lien filed against the LLC or limited partnership's earnings. When profit allocations are made by either entity to their members or partners, a portion would be paid to the judgment creditor to pay down the judgment. Having a charging order placed against an LLC or a limited partnership in many states does not convey voting rights, so creditors cannot take control of the entity and, through that control, reach the assets. In addition, in a situation where the entity is profitable but management decides that the profit needs to be reinvested into the entity, no distributions of profit will be made at all. However, the IRS will consider each member of the LLC (or limited partner, in a limited partnership) to have received their share of the profits and will tax them on those phantom profits accordingly. So for a creditor, not receiving a cash distribution and being taxed on the distribution it did not receive is doubly annoying. Holding real property in either of these entities can be a great deterrent against nuisance litigation and claims.

Should I set up an LLC for each piece of property?

That depends on your comfort level. Remember, the more properties you hold in a single entity, the more you risk your income being affected in the event of a lawsuit. For example, if you hold five rental properties in a single LLC and that LLC is sued by the tenant in property number 3, all of the assets of the LLC could become negatively affected. Many people will prefer to have just one property, not all five, in each LLC, thus limiting the exposure of other assets to any one claim.

At the very least be careful about putting properties from different states into the same LLC. Because the properties are earning income, you will have to register them to do business in each state where property is located, and adhere to local state taxation laws. So, if you have property in a very tax-aggressive state, you may find yourself in a situation where that state attempts to tax your earnings from all of your properties, not just the property located in that state.

Will a land trust give me the asset protection I need?

Not necessarily. A land trust is a great vehicle for privacy because it allows you to name another individual, company, or entity as the trustee, keeping your name off of the public records and keeping the ownership of the land private. However, a land trust is not a corporate entity—it does not have a separate and distinct court-recognized existence—and so you remain personally liable for any injuries, problems, environmental issues, hazardous waste, or other problems related to the property held in the land trust. Even worse, a creditor can reach through and take your interest in a land trust, effectively taking it from you to satisfy a judgment against you. Neither can you claim at trial that you don't own the property held by a land trust. Because you are the beneficial owner of the land trust you are the beneficial owner of the land. However, as mentioned elsewhere in the book, a land trust owned by an LLC offers both privacy and asset protection, and can be a good strategy.

What are the benefits of holding property in a trust as opposed to an LLC?

There are many types of trusts. A living trust is a common estate planning vehicle that offers probate avoidance but no asset protection. In such a case, the real estate is best titled in the name of the LLC with the member interests owned by the living trust. When one party passes away, the LLC membership interests are transferred according to the terms of the trust but the property does not have to be retitled, since the LLC continues to own it.

Another trust is the spendthrift trust, an irrevocable vehicle set up by parents for their children. The assets of the trust may not be reached by later creditors, thus protecting immature and free-spending kids from themselves. Because an independent trustee administers the property until it is distributed, a greater measure of control is achieved. However, overall such trusts pay higher taxes than LLCs and may not be advisable for strong income properties.

Should I put my family home into an LLC?

There can be a loss of tax benefits when you hold your principal residence in something other than your own name. If you move your home into an LLC, it is possible that you will lose the tax-free benefit upon sale. You can also lose the mortgage interest deduction by holding your house in a separate entity.

Most states provide a homestead exemption that protects all or a part of your equity in your home. For example, in Arizona the homestead exemption amount is $100,000. In Florida, it is unlimited. Using the homestead exemption is a much better way to protect your home asset.

Can my company buy my house, then rent it back to me?

Perhaps a better question than "can my?" would be "should my?" In that case, the answer is no for the same reasons that you don't want to transfer the asset into an LLC. You will lose the tax-free gain upon sale.

Can I write off repairs done to my own house?

You cannot deduct the repair costs for your personal residence. But the costs of repairs or improvements for your home office are a deduction.

What can I do with my home office in the basement?

Consider renting that portion of your home to the business as a home office. There needs to be exclusive business purpose on that part of your home (in other words, that space is not merely a part of the dining room) and the space needs to be used in your business. It should be noted that you would only rent and not sell a part of the house to the business. Selling would involve complicated and burdensome title issues.

When a rental property is not rented, can I take that as a loss of income?

The expenses of operating the rental property including the advertising costs are still expenses. You cannot take a loss for lost revenue. You do not pay tax or receive a loss on something you don't receive.

Can I set up a management company to manage my own properties?

Yes. While you cannot be a limited partner or nonmanaging member in an LP or an LLC, respectively, and receive management fees, a separate C corporation, S corporation, or LLC may be established to assume management duties.

Can we use our vacation home as a corporate retreat for our corporation?

Your corporation can pay a fair market value of rent for the time used as a legitimate meeting place.

What can I do to take advantage of more deductions on a business rental property?

Follow the steps outlined in Chapter 6 to identify your current expenses. If the expenses are ordinary and necessary, they are legitimate expenses from income.

I bought an apartment complex yesterday but don't have an LLC set up yet. Is it difficult to transfer title after the fact?

Not particularly. The transfer itself may be done by way of a warranty deed or quit claim deed, which is prepared and filed at the local county recorder's office where the property is located. However, that's the easy part. You may wind up in trouble with your mortgage lender when you transfer the property. Many mortgages have a triggering clause (called a due on sale clause) that requires the entire mortgage to be repaid if title to the property changes hands. Although you are still ultimately the owner of the property, as you own the entity, as far as your bank or lender may be concerned, the property has been transferred and the mortgage repayment clause triggered. Not to mention, a brand-new LLC or limited partnership has no operating history, no assets, and no credit rating. Would you loan $200,000 to an unproven entity in these circumstances?

One way around this is to discuss with your bank or mortgage lender ahead of time your desire to put the property into an entity for estate-planning purposes. You can offer to provide a personal guarantee over the mortgage funds on behalf of your entity. We have found that most banks and mortgage lenders appreciate the words "estate planning" and they appreciate personal guarantees even more. If your bank balks at this, shop around.

What is the best way to protect myself against liability for my rental properties?

We believe that a comprehensive insurance package, combined with holding the entity in an asset-protecting entity such an LLC or a limited partnership, is the best way to go. By holding your rental properties in a good entity, such as an LLC or limited partnership, you can protect yourself personally from claims of tenants or creditors. And, with a good, comprehensive insurance package, you can protect your entity from the claims of others, or from certain disasters such as fire and flooding, and ensure that you will have the money to rebuild, if necessary. Remember Chen and Harmon? Harmon laughed at Chen for spending so much money on comprehensive insurance coverage, but at the end of the day Chen owned both buildings.

If I live in California but own property in Nevada, can I set up a Nevada company?

Absolutely. Nevada has no residency requirements for people or entities who want to use Nevada entities to operate their real estate businesses. However, bear in mind that as a California resident, and assuming you hold your property in a flow-through entity such as an LLC or limited partnership, the income flowing back to you in California will be subject to California state tax, even though it was earned in Nevada.

Assuming my investment property is held in an LLC, can this be given to my spouse upon my death?

Yes. It can be done in many ways, from passing through in your will, being transferred pursuant to a living trust, or by holding your LLC interests as joint tenants with right of survivorship (JTROS). If you choose the JTROS or living trust route, upon your passing away the investment property will automatically be transferred to your spouse or other named beneficiary, saving the problem of having your estate probated before title can be transferred.

What type of repairs are deductible for a rental unit?

Expenses that are incurred to repair an item like fixing a leaky faucet or repairing a handrail on a stairway are deductible in the year paid. Expenses that are incurred that extend the life or improve the property must be capitalized and then depreciated. Examples of capitalizable items would be a complete new roof (as opposed to fixing a hole in the roof) or a room addition.

Are Section 1031 exchanges still done? I heard they stopped doing them in 1986.

Section 1031 like-kind exchanges are still very much done in the real estate world. They are a terrific way to defer tax from the sale of a piece of investment property.

What are the benefits of an LLC compared to an LP for holding real estate?

The LLC provides for limited liability for all owners (members) whereas a LP only has limited liability for the limited partner. The general partner of an LP would have full liability. This can be easily overcome by forming a second corporation or LLC to serve as the general partner.

Can I write off the interest for more than one mortgage in a calendar year?

Absolutely! The IRS practices a matching program for Form 1098s that are prepared by mortgage companies and banks to report mortgage interest. Make sure that you report the same amount on your tax return that is shown on these forms. If there are changes to the amount reported, make that change on a different line item with an attached statement explaining the change.

Do I have to have a real estate license to be considered a real estate professional?

No, you do not need to be a licensed real estate agent in order to be considered a real estate professional. The test for real estate professional status relates to the hours you work in the real estate capacity in proportion to other work you do. If you work more hours in real estate activities, and a minimum of 750 hours per year, then you likely qualify as a real estate professional.

My wife and I are both retired. Are there any benefits if both of us become real estate professionals?

The real estate professional designation of a taxpayer allows the taxpayer to fully take all real estate losses against other income. If you and your wife file a joint return, then only one of you need qualify as a real estate professional in order to take advantage of this provision. There is no tax advantage, but you might find it is very rewarding to investigate real estate together!

Can I write real estate losses off from one piece of property against the income of another?

As long as both properties are similar, such as both are rental properties in which you actively participate, then the loss against one can offset the income from another. If they are dissimilar, such as in the case of a motel operation (which is considered an active trade or business) and a piece of property held for future development, they cannot offset.

Where can I get a list of personal property items included in a rental property that can be depreciated at an accelerated rate?

Personal property items can be depreciated at five to fifteen years as opposed to the twenty-seven and a half to thirty-nine years required for real property. The current list of accepted personal property items and their depreciable lives can be found at www.taxloopholes.com.

Where can I learn about the eviction laws in various states?

You can access this information at www.successdna.com.

At what point should I consider forming an LLC or LP to hold my properties?

Preferably before acquiring the real estate, since you will want title to be held in the name of the LLC or LP. If you already own real estate you should take the steps to form an LLC or LP posthaste. Information on this process can be obtained at www.sutlaw.com.

Appendix B
Useful Real Estate Checklists

A review of the information on these checklists as it relates to your transaction will provide you with the background necessary to either walk away or purchase with confidence. Please note that these checklists are not intended to be comprehensive, nor applicable to every transaction; rather, they should serve as starting points for your own due diligence review.

Buyer Disclosure Checklist
Owner Information

- ☐ Name, address, phone number, business number
- ☐ Reason for selling
- ☐ Occupation
- ☐ If owner broker/agent

Loan Information

- ☐ Name/address of lender
- ☐ Is current loan assumable? If yes, with or without qualification?
- ☐ Name title vested in
- ☐ Loan number
- ☐ Asking price
- ☐ Assessed value of property
- ☐ Interest rate
- ☐ Closing costs
- ☐ Current loan amount/dates

- ☐ Balance of current loan
- ☐ Is loan assumable?
- ☐ Discounts available for loan prepayment?
- ☐ If second can be discounted, if any
- ☐ If balloon payment/amount due/when

- ☐ If prepayment penalty
- ☐ Will seller help finance/pay points?
- ☐ Yearly tax amount
- ☐ New loan amount
- ☐ Length of loan
- ☐ Monthly payment amount
- ☐ Insurance costs/requirements
- ☐ Home guarantee?
- ☐ CC&Rs (covenants, conditions, restrictions)
- ☐ Move-in date
- ☐ How long on market
- ☐ If previously listed/length of time

Fees

- ☐ Application
- ☐ Appraisal
- ☐ Loan fee
- ☐ Inspections/pest, structure
- ☐ Recording fee

- ☐ Credit report
- ☐ Escrow fee
- ☐ Points
- ☐ Title report/insurance
- ☐ Insurance

Property

- ☐ Legal description of property
- ☐ Zoning of property
- ☐ Proximity of schools
- ☐ Extent of landscaping
- ☐ Sprinkler system/type
- ☐ Inspection report/environmental concerns

- ☐ Square footage of lot
- ☐ Location of property
- ☐ Easy access to shopping
- ☐ Size of yards/front and back
- ☐ Fences/condition of

Building

- ☐ Age of structure
- ☐ Number of stories

- ☐ Type and condition of roof

- ☐ Number of rooms
- ☐ Square footage of structure
- ☐ Condition of wiring
- ☐ Gas or electric heating/condition of
- ☐ Alarm system? Owned or leased? If leased, will it remain in home after sale?
- ☐ Kitchen amenities/condition of
- ☐ Utility costs/heating costs
- ☐ Condition of carpeting
- ☐ Number of bathrooms
- ☐ Inventory of what included/ draperies, etc.
- ☐ Garage/size/condition

- ☐ What kind of view

- ☐ Builder
- ☐ Condition and type of construction inside and outside
- ☐ Inspection report of structure/ termites, etc.
- ☐ Number of bedrooms
- ☐ Condition of plumbing
- ☐ Condition of foundation
- ☐ Air conditioning/condition of
- ☐ If fireplace/condition of? Has the chimney been cleaned recently?

- ☐ Gas or electric appliances/water heater
- ☐ What kind of flooring
- ☐ Number of bedrooms/square footage
- ☐ Other rooms/description/condition of
- ☐ Number of windows/condition of

- ☐ Insulation up to code/storm windows, doors
- ☐ Any needed repairs

Seller Disclosure Checklist
General/Legal

- ☐ Home insurance
- ☐ Previous pest inspection reports
- ☐ Any additions to building made by current and past owners? Were additions properly permitted?
- ☐ Restrictions on property
- ☐ Easements on property
- ☐ Anyone having right of first refusal or option to buy
- ☐ Known future problems affecting property
- ☐ Property owned near this property

- ☐ Previous inspection reports
- ☐ Year structure built
- ☐ Pending legal actions

- ☐ Liens against property/explain
- ☐ Is property leased?/when expire
- ☐ Known conditions affecting property

- ☐ Pending expansion/real estate development of area
- ☐ Problems with stability of ground beneath property, settling, cracks in cement/describe

- ☐ Property in designated zone/flood, hazard, etc., area

Roof

- ☐ Condition
- ☐ How old
- ☐ Any problems/leakage/date

- ☐ Composition
- ☐ Any repair/resurfacing/date

Heating/Electrical

- ☐ Date heating system installed

- ☐ Condition of heating system
- ☐ Manner of ventilation/describe
- ☐ Insulation up to code?
- ☐ Available voltage
- ☐ Date of last inspection/service

- ☐ Kind of heating system/make—gas or electric
- ☐ Previous heating inspections/date
- ☐ Acceptable ventilation
- ☐ Condition of electrical equipment
- ☐ Known defects/describe

Water/Sewer

- ☐ Water supply source/city, septic tank
- ☐ Condition of water supply
- ☐ Known prior plumbing leaks/rust problems
- ☐ Any flooding/date, how repaired
- ☐ Drainage problems/describe

- ☐ Type of water pipes
- ☐ Any water pressure problems
- ☐ Known standing water areas

- ☐ Adequate drainage/roof, ground
- ☐ Water heater/condition/age

- [ ] Capacity of water heater
- [ ] Location of water heater
- [ ] What company did inspection
- [ ] Condition of landscape sprinklers/describe

- [ ] Water heater/safety/pressure release valve
- [ ] Water heater last date inspected and/or serviced
- [ ] Safety device for water heater

Commercial Property Due Diligence Checklist
Objective

- [ ] Estate building
- [ ] Tax shelter
- [ ] Other/description

- [ ] Equity return
- [ ] Spendable income/amount

Background Search

- [ ] Better Business Bureau
- [ ] Lending institution

- [ ] Chamber of Commerce
- [ ] Utility companies

Owner Information

- [ ] Name, address
- [ ] Bank reference
- [ ] Owner occupying property
- [ ] Attorney/legal status
- [ ] Amount of capital
- [ ] Date business was started
- [ ] Reason for selling
- [ ] Previously listed/price/time on market

- [ ] Business phone/residence phone
- [ ] Occupation tax bracket
- [ ] Tax accountant
- [ ] Broker or real estate agent
- [ ] Annual gross income
- [ ] Operating statements for years in business
- [ ] How long on market

Lease

- [ ] Lessee's name
- [ ] Time left on original lease/option to renew/rent increased
- [ ] Rent based on percentage/ how computed
- [ ] Paid monthly/yearly
- [ ] Tax clause in lease
- [ ] Get copies of lease/agreements

- [ ] Type of lease/original or sublease
- [ ] Method of computing rent
- [ ] Rent based on square footage/ building only or frontage included
- [ ] Option to buy/renew/first refusal
- [ ] Who performs maintenance/interior, exterior, landscaping
- [ ] Copies of contracts/management

Loan

- ☐ Type of loan/loan number
- ☐ Name title vested in
- ☐ Assessed value of property
- ☐ Assumable loan/transferable

- ☐ Will seller help finance?
- ☐ Balance of original loan/ date reported
- ☐ Any liens on property
- ☐ Prepayment penalty

- ☐ Interest rate
- ☐ Lender name and address
- ☐ Type of new loan/dates
- ☐ Can second loan be bought at discount? Amount of discount?
- ☐ Original amount loaned/date
- ☐ Balloon payment?/amount due/when

- ☐ Interest rate locked in?/time
- ☐ Preliminary title report

Building

- ☐ Age of building
- ☐ Condition of basement/foundations
- ☐ How building constructed

- ☐ Square footage

- ☐ Architectural design
- ☐ Exterior finish and condition
- ☐ Adequately view from street or parking lot

Building Interior

- ☐ Number of floors in building
- ☐ Efficient design of space
- ☐ Number of windows
- ☐ Adequate lighting
- ☐ Condition of floors
- ☐ Condition/age of wiring
- ☐ Condition/age of air conditioning

- ☐ Security patrol/burglar alarms installed
- ☐ Inventory included/description, estimate of value

- ☐ Condition of space
- ☐ Ceiling height
- ☐ Condition of windows
- ☐ Toilet location and number
- ☐ Adequate wiring
- ☐ Condition/age of heating system
- ☐ Fire protection/overhead sprinklers/ number and location
- ☐ Number and condition of locks

Service Costs

- ☐ Services provided by shopping center
- ☐ Water/garbage
- ☐ Security
- ☐ Equipment cost/rental cost, depreciation
- ☐ Accounting/legal fees

- ☐ Heating/air conditioning
- ☐ Electric/gas
- ☐ Insurance
- ☐ Advertising costs

Property

☐ Legal description
☐ Restrictions
☐ Covenants/conditions/restrictions
☐ Square footage of property lot
☐ Room to expand
☐ List of repairs needed
☐ Adequate parking
☐ Condition of parking lot

☐ Survey report
☐ Zoning restrictions
☐ Map of area showing property plot
☐ Storefront footage
☐ Inspection report of property
☐ Landscaping/condition of
☐ Adequate loading area

Location of Property

☐ Easy access to building

☐ Foot traffic in front of building
☐ Population within range of business
☐ Condition of streets/neighborhood
☐ Nearest closely related business

☐ Closeness to main roads/freeway/
bus line
☐ Area traffic patterns
☐ Estimated income/size of area families
☐ Estimated area population growth
☐ Category of shopping center

Environmental Due Diligence Checklist
Documents to Review

☐ Lot description/square footage
☐ Primary use description
☐ Regulations/requirements—local,
state, federal
☐ Complaints by citizens

☐ Contracts with disposal services,
waste transport
☐ Insurance coverage/claims for
environmental loss with resolution
☐ Pending litigation
☐ Judgments, settlement agreements

☐ Building description
☐ Operating permits
☐ Maps, aerial photos, diagrams,
technical reports
☐ Environmental assessments, Phase I
and Phase II reports
☐ Reports on produced pollutants

☐ Description of noncompliance
penalties
☐ Environmental violations

Environmental Information with Descriptions

☐ Standard Industrial Classification
number
☐ Manner disposed of
☐ Spillage of waste
☐ Underground tanks
☐ Records of spills/accidents

☐ Hazardous waste on property

☐ Recycling done
☐ Stored materials
☐ Known leaks
☐ Known contamination to water or
ground on this property

□ Claims against company for
  shipping waste   □ Prior claims against owner

□ Water pollution history   □ All permits

□ Last site check

Reports/Permits/Citations

□ Ownership history/detail   □ Hazardous Material Site
                                         characterization

□ Geotechnical   □ Air quality

□ Water quality   □ Department of Health Services

□ Sanitation Department   □ Environmental Protection Agency

Setting

□ Type of soil   □ Vegetation—healthy?

□ Soil stains   □ Ground water depth

□ Destination of surface water runoff

On-Site Facilities Used for/Description and
Storage of Chemicals Used

Businesses of:

□ Dry cleaning   □ Gas station

□ Plant nursery   □ Paint/repair of automobiles

Manufacturing, storing, etc. of:

□ Copiers   □ Semiconductors/electrical devices

□ Glue/rubber products   □ Detergent/soap

□ Pesticides/fertilizer   □ Paper products/pulp

□ Furniture/wood preservatives   □ Jewelry/metal plating or products

□ Plastics/foams   □ Petroleum products

□ Chemicals/explosives   □ Paint

□ Glass   □ Auto parts

Diane Kennedy

Diane Kennedy, C.P.A., is the co-author of Real Estate LoopHoles and the author of the best-seller LoopHoles of the Rich – How the Rich Legally Make More Money and Pay Less Tax in the Rich Dad's Advisor's series. She is also the founder and co-owner of DKA (D Kennedy & Assoc), DKAdvisors and TaxCents as well as numerous real estate investment companies. Through all of these companies, Diane has built her reputation by empowering and educating others about the tax loopholes legally available to all individuals.

For over twenty years, Diane has assisted individuals and corporations from small business owners to real estate investors in strategically structuring their businesses to take advantage of the tax loopholes available. Her firm specializes in innovative tax planning that minimizes tax liability and maximizes legal protection along with educating and empowering individuals to make financial decisions.

Diane is highly respected within the accounting profession as the co-author of two college textbooks on accounting and computer topics and a book regarding corporate tax. She has authored numerous tax-related articles and has served as a past instructor at the University of Nevada, Reno. She was selected as a lecturer on U.S. tax laws to the People's Republic of China. Her notes are now part of the official documentation used in Beijing, China. She is a past recipient of the prestigious Blue Chip Enterprise award given to the business owner demonstrating the most entrepreneurial spirit in the State of Nevada. She is also a past recipient of the National Chamber of Commerce award for Excellence in Business. She has been featured on CNN, CNNfn, Bloomberg TV and radio, CNBC, StockTalkAmerica and numerous local TV and radio shows. She is also a co-host of the nationally syndicated radio show WealthTalkAmerica.

Diane is an outspoken proponent of proactive tax planning allowing individuals and corporations to keep more of what they make. She is perhaps best known for her work with Robert Kiyosaki, as one of his selective Rich Dad's Advisor. She knows the secrets that the rich use to reduce their taxes and, with basic and simple understanding, discloses those secrets to everyone.

Diane Kennedy can be reached through her website at www.taxloopholes.com.

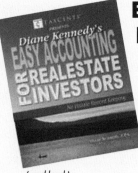

Garrett Sutton

Garrett Sutton, Esq., is the author of the best-seller, Own Your Own Corporation and How To Buy and Sell a Business, and co-author with Diane Kennedy of Real Estate Loopholes - all books in the Rich Dad's Advisor series. He is an attorney with over twenty years of experience in assisting individuals and businesses to determine their appropriate corporate structure, limit their liability, protect their assets, and advance their financial, real estate, and personal goals.

Garrett and his law firm represent hundreds of corporations, limited liability companies, limited partnerships, and individuals in their business-related law matters, including incorporation, contracts, mergers and acquisitions, private and public company securities offerings, and ongoing business-related legal advice.

Garrett attended Colorado College and the University of California at Berkeley, where he received a B.S. in business administration in 1975. He graduated with a J.D. in 1978 from Hastings College of the Law, the University of California's law school in San Francisco. He is the founder of SuccessDNA, Inc., which assists entrepreneurs in achieving their goals.

Garrett is a member of the State Bar of Nevada, the State Bar of California, and the American Bar Association. He has written numerous professional articles and serves on the Publication Committee of the State Bar of Nevada. He is also the author of How To Use Limited Liability Companies and Limited Partnerships (SuccessDNA). He has been quoted in the Wall Street Journal and in other national and local business publications. He is also a co-host of the Nationally Syndicated Radio Show, Wealth Talk America.

Garrett enjoys speaking with entrepreneurs on the advantages of forming business entities, asset protection and business and real estate strategies. He is a frequent lecturer for the Nevada Microenterprise Institute and the Small Business Administration, as well as with the Rich Dad's Advisor Series.

Garrett serves on the board of the American Baseball Foundation, located in Birmingham, Alabama, as well as the Reno, Nevada-based Tech Alliance.

For more information on Garrett Sutton and his firm, please visit his website at www.sutlaw.com.

How Can I Protect My Real Estate Assets?

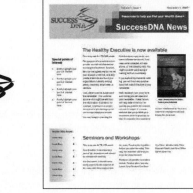

Robert Kiyosaki's Edumercial
An Educational Commercial

The Three Incomes

In the world of accounting, there are three different types of income: earned, passive and portfolio. When my real dad said to me, "Go to school, get good grades and find a safe secure job," he was recommending I work for earned income. When my rich dad said, "The rich don't work for money, they have their money work for them," he was talking about passive income and portfolio income. Passive income, in most cases, is derived from real estate investments. Portfolio income is income derived from paper assets, such as stocks, bonds, and mutual funds.

Rich dad used to say, "The key to becoming wealthy is the ability to convert earned income into passive income and/or portfolio income as quickly as possible." He would say, "The taxes are highest on earned income. The least taxed income is passive income. That is another reason why you want your money working hard for you. The government taxes the income you work hard for more than the income your money works hard for."

The Key to Financial Freedom

The key to financial freedom and great wealth is a person's ability or skill to convert earned income into passive income and/or portfolio income. That is the skill that my rich dad spent a lot of time teaching Mike and me. Having that skill is the reason my wife Kim and I are financially free, never needing to work again. We continue to work because we choose to. Today we own a real estate investment company for passive income and participate in private placements and initial public offerings of stock for portfolio income.

Investing to become rich requires a different set of personal skills, skills essential for financial success as well as low-risk and high-investment returns. In other words, knowing how to create assets that buy other assets. The problem is that gaining the basic education and experience required is often time consuming, frightening, and expensive, especially when you make mistakes with your own money. That is why I created the patented education board games trademarked as CASHFLOW®.

CASHFLOW® 101

CASHFLOW 101 is an educational program that teaches accounting, finance, and investing at the same time and makes learning fun.

Learn how to get out of the rat race and onto the fast track where your money works for you instead of you working hard for your money. The educational program, CASHFLOW 101, includes three audiocassettes which reveal distinctions on CASHFLOW 101 as well as valuable investment information and a video titled "The Secrets of the Rich."

CASHFLOW 101 is recommended for adults and children age 10 and older.

CASHFLOW® 202

CASHFLOW 202 teaches you the advanced business and investing techniques used by technical investors by adding volatility to the game. It teaches the advanced investment techniques of "short-selling stock," "put-options," "call-options," "straddles" and real estate exchanges.

You must have CASHFLOW 101 in order to play CASHFLOW 202. This package contains new game sheets, new playing cards, and 4 audiocassettes.

CASHFLOW for KIDS™

Give your children the financial head start necessary to thrive in today's fast-paced and changing world. Schools teach children how to work for money. CASHFLOW for Kids teaches children how to have money work for them.

CASHFLOW for Kids is a complete educational package which includes the book and audiocassette titled "Rich Dad's Guide to Raising Your Child's Financial I.Q."

CASHFLOW for Kids is recommended for children ages 6 and older.

RICH KID SMART KID

RichKidSmartKid.com is an innovative and interactive website designed to convey key concepts about money and finance in ways that are fun and challenging — and educational for young people in grades K through 12.

YOU CAN MAKE A DIFFERENCE
How?

Play CASHFLOW for Kids™ with family and friends and share the RichKidSmartKid.com website with your local teachers and school administrators.

We'll do the rest!

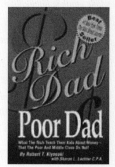
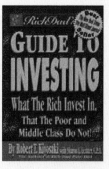

Rich Dad's Rich Kid Smart Kid

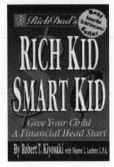

Give your child a financial headstart. Awaken your child's love of learning how to be financially free. Imagine the results you'll see when they start early!

This book is written for parents who value education, want to give their child a financial and academic headstart in life, and are willing to take an active role to make it happen. Rich Kid Smart Kid is designed to help you give your child the same inspiring and practical financial knowledge that Robert's rich dad gave him. Learn how to awaken your child's love of learning.

Rich Dad's Retire Young Retire Rich

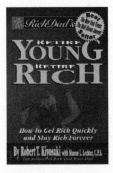

A powerful personal story about how Robert and Kim Kiyosaki started with nothing, and retired financially free in less than 10 years. If you do not plan on working hard all your life, this book is for you.

If you're tired of the same old investment advice—such as "be patient," "invest for the long term," and "diversify"—then this book is for you.

Robert explains in detail the power of leverage. How to leverage your mind, your financial plans, your actions and most importantly, your first steps to becoming financially free.

You will learn Rich Dad's techniques using leverage to first build financial security and ultimately have the life you want.

Rich Dad's Prophecy

Why the Biggest Stock Market Crash in History Is Still Coming...and How You Can Prepare Yourself and Profit from It!

In the 6th book of the Rich Dad Series, Robert Kiyosaki predicts the inevitable financial crisis that will hit the U.S. when 83 million baby boomers retire, taking with them such a vast amount of savings that the market is sure to crumble. And that doesn't even take into account the already wobbly state of the stock market, as blue chip companies go under, sending the Dow plummeting. But Rich Dad's Prophecy is not a "doom and gloom" book, it's a "doom and boom" book, with sure-fire strategies designed to avoid disaster in the coming crisis.

Protecting Your #1 Asset - Creating Fortunes From Your Ideas. An Intellectual Property Handbook

Protecting your #1 Asset will teach you how to turn your ideas into intellectual property assets, avoid inadvertently giving away your rights, use intellectual property to build barriers to competition and generate cash flow by licensing your intellectual property to others.

by Michael Lechter, Esq.

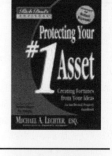

SalesDogs - You Do Not Have To Be An Attack Dog To Be Successful In Sales.

SalesDogs will introduce five breeds of Sales Dogs which will allow you to make more money by playing to your natural strengths. Reveal the five simple but critical revenue-generating skills to create endless streams of qualified buyers and life-long sales and teach you how to radically change your attitude in thirty seconds or less so you can direct your financial results.

by Blair Singer

LoopHoles Of The Rich - How The Rich Legally Make More Money And Pay Less Taxes.

LoopHoles of the Rich will reveal how to control how much tax you pay and when you pay it, condense 500,000+ pages of IRS Tax law into 3 easy rules that keep money in your pocket and how to find the right business structure for your business to pay less tax and protect what you have.

by Diane Kennedy, C.P.A.

Own Your Own Corporation - Why The Rich Own Their Own Companies And Everyone Else Works For Them.

Own Your Own Corporation illustrates how to:

- Select the best entity for your own personal strategy
- Raise money for your new venture
- Maximize the incredible benefits of a C corporation
- Use employment agreements for your benefit
- Use Nevada corporations for asset protection and tax savings
- Easily prepare and maintain corporate records

by Garrett Sutton, Esq.

Real Estate Riches - How To Become Rich Using Your Banker's Money.

Real Estate Riches will:
- Show you why real estate is tens and hundreds of times better than other investments
- Train you how to find the 'Deal of the Decade' - every week
- Teach you how to massively increase the value of a property without spending much money
- Explain how the tax man can subsidize your real estate investment
- Reveal how to create passive income using your banker's money so that you only work if you want to

by Dolf de Roos, Ph.D.

How To Buy And Sell A Business - How You Can Win In The Business Quadrant.

How To Buy And Sell A Business reveals the strategies used by successful entrepreneurs to acquire and cash out business investments. Written in a clear and easily understandable style, How To Buy And Sell A Business provides the necessary knowledge to avoid the pitfalls and overcome the obstacles in order to achieve a winning transaction.

by Garrett Sutton, Esq.

Real Estate LoopHoles - Secrets Of Successful Real Estate Investing.

Real Estate LoopHoles will reveal how to use tax loopholes to your advantage and stop others from using legal loopholes to take your assets. In addition, you will learn to:
- Determine the best way to hold title to your real estate investments
- Use your own home as a tax free money-making venture
- Use the Seven Tax Loopholes only available to real estate owners
- Protect your real estate assets from tenants and creditors

by Diane Kennedy, C.P.A. and Garrett Sutton, Esq.

Rich Dad's
STRAIGHT TALK

Rich Dad's You Can Choose To Be Rich

Rich Dad's 6 Steps to Becoming a Successful Real Estate Ivestor

How To Increase The Income from Your Real Estate Investments – *The Secrets of Professional Property Managers*

Join Rich Dad's Community at
www.richdad.com
and share your adventure with thousands of others worldwide. Embarking on Rich Dad's Journey is the first step to a life free from the fear and worry of not having enough money. It's the first step in becoming part of a community of individuals who are committed to change and become financially free.

To order books visit: www.twbookmark.com

For more information:
CASHFLOW® Technologies, Inc.
4330 N. Civic Center Plaza, Suite 101
Scottsdale, Arizona 85251 USA
(800) 308-3585 or (480) 998-6971
Fax: (480) 348-1349
e-mail: info@richdad.com

Australia/New Zealand:
Rich Dad Australia
4-6 Mentmore Avenue
Rosebery NSW 2018 Australia
TEL: 1300 660 020 • FAX: 1300 301 988
email: info@richdad.com.au